THE SHAWNEES
AND THE
WAR FOR AMERICA

THE PENGUIN LIBRARY OF AMERICAN INDIAN HISTORY

THE
SHAWNEES
AND THE
WAR FOR AMERICA

COLIN G. CALLOWAY

THE PENGUIN LIBRARY
OF AMERICAN INDIAN HISTORY

VIKING

VIKING

Published by the Penguin Group

Penguin Group (USA) Inc., 375 Hudson Street, New York, New York 10014,
U.S.A. • Penguin Group (Canada), 90 Eglinton Avenue East, Suite 700, Toronto,
Ontario, Canada M4P 2Y3 (a division of Pearson Penguin Canada Inc.) • Penguin
Books Ltd, 80 Strand, London WC2R 0RL, England • Penguin Ireland,
25 St Stephen's Green, Dublin 2, Ireland (a division of Penguin Books Ltd) •
Penguin Books Australia Ltd, 250 Camberwell Road, Camberwell, Victoria 3124,
Australia (a division of Pearson Australia Group Pty Ltd) • Penguin Books India
Pvt Ltd, 11 Community Centre, Panchsheel Park, New Delhi - 110 017, India •
Penguin Group (NZ), 67 Apollo Drive, Rosedale, North Shore 0745, Auckland, New
Zealand (a division of Pearson New Zealand Ltd) • Penguin Books (South Africa)
(Pty) Ltd, 24 Sturdee Avenue, Rosebank, Johannesburg 2196, South Africa

Penguin Books Ltd, Registered Offices: 80 Strand, London WC2R 0RL, England

First published in 2007 by Viking Penguin, a member of Penguin Group (USA) Inc.

1   3   5   7   9   10   8   6   4   2

Copyright © Colin G. Calloway, 2007
All rights reserved

ISBN: 978-0-670-03862-6

Printed in the United Stares of America
Set in Granjon
Designed by Katy Riegel

For Marcia, Graeme, and Meg, as always

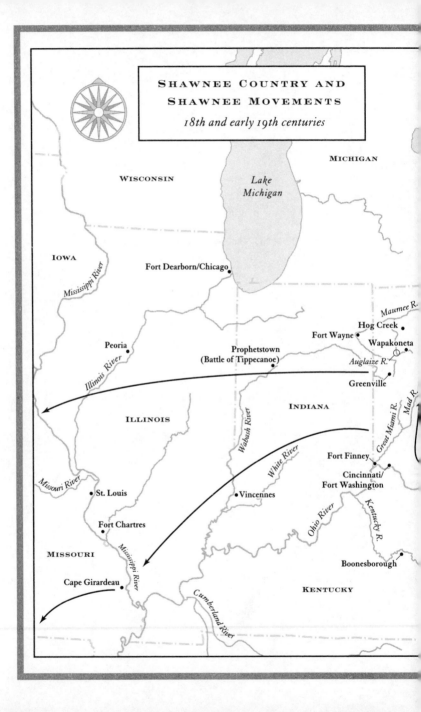

SHAWNEE COUNTRY AND
SHAWNEE MOVEMENTS

18th and early 19th centuries

MICHIGAN

WISCONSIN

Lake Michigan

IOWA

Mississippi River

Fort Dearborn/Chicago

Maumee R.

Hog Creek

Fort Wayne

Wapakoneta

Auglaize R.

Peoria

Prophetstown
(Battle of Tippecanoe)

Illinois River

Greenville

Mad R.

ILLINOIS

INDIANA

Wabash River

White River

Great Miami R.

Fort Finney

Cincinnati/
Fort Washington

Missouri River

St. Louis

Vincennes

Fort Chartres

Mississippi River

Ohio River

Kentucky R.

MISSOURI

Boonesborough

Cape Girardeau

KENTUCKY

Cumberland River

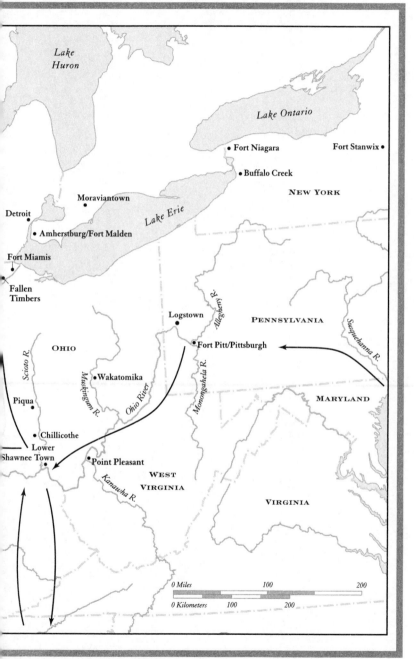

CONTENTS

Contents

Contents

8

REMOVALS AND SURVIVALS

155

AFTERWORD

174

THE SHAWNEES AND
THEIR NEIGHBORS

Shawnees: The principal divisions of the Shawnees and their traditional responsibilities as described by Thomas Wildcat Alford (1860–1938). Spellings vary.

Chillicothe and *Thawekila:* The two principal divisions, responsible for political affairs and matters affecting the whole tribe; generally supplied the principal tribal chiefs.

Mekoche: Provided health, medicine, and food; healers and counselors.

Pekowi: Responsible for maintaining order and for matters of religion and ritual.

Kispoko: Took the lead in preparing and training for war and supplying war chiefs.

NORTHEAST

Delawares or *Lenni Lenape:* Spoke dialects of the Algonquian language. Originally located in what is now New Jersey and eastern Pennsylvania, like the Shawnees they moved westward piecemeal, into the Ohio country in the eighteenth century and beyond to Kansas, Oklahoma, and other locations in the nineteenth century.

Iroquois or *Six Nations:* In their own language, the *Hodenausonee,* or People of the Longhouse. The *Mohawks, Oneidas, Onondagas, Cayugas, Senecas,* and *Tuscaroras* constituted the Iroquois League stretching across upstate New York.

Mahicans: Algonquian-speaking people who originally inhabited the Hudson Valley and parts of western Massachusetts.

Nanticokes: Originally located on the eastern shore of Chesapeake Bay in what is now southern Maryland. Some moved to Pennsylvania in the mid–eighteenth century, and by the end of the century some lived close to the Delawares and Shawnees in Ohio.

GREAT LAKES/OHIO COUNTRY

Hurons: Called themselves *Wendat*; spoke a northern Iroquoian language. Before the mid–seventeenth century, formed a confederacy of several tribes around Georgian Bay on the northeast edge of Lake Huron, living in longhouses and farming extensive cornfields. May have numbered as many as thirty thousand before epidemics hit and they were dispersed by Iroquois attacks in 1648–49.

Illinois: Sometimes referred to as the Illinois confederacy; a dozen related Algonquian groups, including the *Kaskaskias*, *Cahokias*, *Peorias*, and others.

Kickapoos: Algonquian-speaking people. Like the Shawnees, with whom they are often said to be related, they experienced a history of recurrent movement. By the mid–eighteenth century they were living in Illinois and Indiana, and along the Wabash. In the nineteenth century, they migrated west of the Mississippi to Missouri, Kansas, Oklahoma, and Texas, and some relocated to Mexico.

Mascoutens: Semisedentary Algonquian tribe located in what is now Michigan and Wisconsin; closely connected to their Kickapoo neighbors.

Miamis: Algonquian-speaking people living in the Wabash Valley in Indiana and reaching into western Ohio.

Mingos: Primarily Senecas and Cayugas who took up residence in the Ohio country in the eighteenth century.

Ojibwas: Algonguian people living all around the Great Lakes but particularly in what is now Ontario and Michigan. Sometimes called *Chippewa* or *Ojibway*, in their own language,

Anishinabeg: Together with the Potawatomis and Ottawas, they formed the Three Fires Confederacy.

Ottawas: Renowned as traders; lived mainly in what is now Michigan.

Potawatomis: Lived around the southern end of Lake Michigan in the area around what is now Chicago.

Sauks and *Foxes:* Related tribes living on the upper Mississippi River in what is now Illinois and Wisconsin.

Winnebagos: A Siouan-speaking people, they call themselves *Ho-Chunk*; inhabited the western Great Lakes, primarily in what is now Wisconsin.

Wyandots: A group of Hurons who moved into the area around what is now Detroit after the Huron confederacy was destroyed in the mid–seventeenth century, and then into northern Ohio in the eighteenth century.

Southeast

Catawbas: Siouan-speaking people inhabiting the South Carolina piedmont.

Cherokees: One of the most populous southeastern nations, divided into several geographical regions and inhabiting towns in the mountains and foothills of Georgia, the western Carolinas, and eastern Tennessee. Like most of the southeastern tribes, they were agriculturalists. Spoke an Iroquoian language but often in conflict with the Iroquois of New York.

Chickamaugas: A group of Cherokees who split off from the parent tribe and relocated to western Tennessee during the American Revolution.

Chickasaws: Relatively small tribe inhabiting northern Mississippi and western Tennessee. Culturally and linguistically related to the Choctaws but sometimes fought against them. They raided for slaves and earned a formidable reputation as warriors.

Choctaws: Numerous people inhabiting forty to fifty towns in the river valleys of what is now central Mississippi. Their numbers and strategic location in the southern Mississippi Valley meant they were courted as allies by European colonial powers.

Creeks: A loose confederacy of some fifty autonomous towns and including several distinct languages, located in Georgia and Alabama. Shawnees lived near the Creeks when they were in the South and often maintained close relations with them.

Seminoles: People who moved away from the Creek confederacy in the eighteenth century and took up residence in Florida, where they developed a separate identity.

Westos: Migrated from the north to the Savannah River, where the Shawnees met them in the seventeenth century. Raided neighboring tribes for slaves, whom they sold to the English colonies.

Yamassees: Name applied to several groups who migrated north from Florida and settled on the Savannah River in Georgia in the seventeenth century. Defeated by the English in the Yamassee War of 1715–17, many retreated back to Florida.

West

Caddos: Members of several loose confederacies; farming societies that inhabited villages in the Red River region of Texas, Arkansas, and Louisiana.

Comanches: By the time the Shawnees met them in Texas, the Comanches had developed an economy and culture based on horses and buffalo-hunting and established themselves as the dominant Indian power on the southern plains.

Osages: Siouan-speaking people with a reputation as fierce warriors; they dominated the area between the Missouri and Arkansas rivers in the eighteenth century.

Quapaws: Also known to the French as *Arkansas*; inhabited villages in what is today eastern Arkansas.

INTRODUCTION

IN JANUARY 1773 Reverend David Jones crossed the Scioto River and entered Shawnee country. A Baptist minister and army chaplain, Jones had set out to bring the word of God to the Indians living west of the Ohio River. Passing Piqua, a Shawnee community of about one hundred people and a "most remarkable town for robbers and villains," he hurried on to another Shawnee town, Blue Jacket's Town, which he described as "peaceable." There he ate breakfast with Kishanosity, a civil chief the English called Hardman. Kishanosity listened politely to what he had to say and seemed willing to learn about God. Jones pronounced him "a man of good sense." He got a rather different reception at Chillicothe, the principal Shawnee town located on a large plain covered in cornfields next to a branch of Paint Creek. On the first day of

February, a chief named Othaawaapeelethee, or Yellow Hawk, came to see Jones. "This Indian . . . esteems himself as a great speaker and very wise," wrote Jones, "and this may be justly said of him, that he is saucy enough." Speaking through an interpreter, Yellow Hawk asked Jones what was his "business among them; for he understood that I was no trader." Jones replied "that my chief business was to instruct them from God." Yellow Hawk said he suspected as much and launched into a long speech, "not with a very pleasant countenance, nor the most agreeable tone of voice." "When God, who at first made us all, prescribed our way of living, he allowed white people to live one way, and Indians another," said Yellow Hawk. He refused to listen to Jones "on the subject of religion, for he was resolved not to believe what might be said, nor pay any regard to it. And he believed it would be the mind of the other Indians." The Shawnees "had lived a long time as they do now, and liked it very well," said Yellow Hawk; "he and his people would live as they had done." When Jones tried to argue his case, Yellow Hawk became angry. Jones decided discretion was the better part of valor and backed off.[1]

The encounter in many ways exemplified the history of Shawnee dealings with Europeans and Americans. In the struggle over land and culture that lies at the heart of America's story, the Shawnees earned a reputation for stiff resistance against encroachment on their territory and for staunch defense of their way of life. David Jones's experience at Chilli-

cothe was not an isolated incident: he told Moravian missionary
David Zeisberger he met a similar reception in five Shawnee
towns that winter. He "did not find one person who was in-
quiring about God" and was not allowed to speak privately
with Shawnees, "much less to preach a single time." In the
end, he had to flee for his life. "He said he would certainly
never go into that area again because that is not how he had
imagined things would be."[2] Another Shawnee chief, Gischenatsi, fended off missionary Zeisberger's overtures at the village of Wakatomika in the fall. The Moravians won many
converts among the neighboring Delawares, but not among
the Shawnees, who saw missionaries as wolves in sheep's
clothing. Men like Zeisberger, said Gischenatsi, always
claimed "to have great wisdom and understanding from
above," but their real purpose was to "deceive the Indians, to
defraud them of their lands." They regarded the Indians as
fools but the Shawnees would not be fooled. Some Shawnees
listened politely, but like Jones, Zeisberger got nowhere. He
was not surprised, he confided to his diary: "I really see now
that it could not have turned out any other way, because this is
the border and Satan is resisting and watching to see that we
do not come further into his territory."[3]

In a way, Zeisberger was right. Shawnee country *was* a
border, although Shawnee men and women, not Satan, defended it. They fought for their lands, their freedom, and the
right to live their own ways of life. The Shawnees are not as

famous as their more numerous neighbors, the Iroquois to the north in what is now New York State and the Cherokees to the south in the Carolinas, Tennessee, and Georgia. Yet even their enemies grudgingly acknowledged the Shawnees' tenacity and courage—"a brave little Tribe," according to one account.[4] For more than sixty years, they stood in the front lines, waging a war of territorial and cultural resistance that ranged across the present-day states of Pennsylvania, West Virginia, Kentucky, Ohio, Indiana, and Missouri. As one Shawnee leader told the British, "We have always been the frontier."[5]

The war primarily concerned land. The one-thousand-mile-long Ohio River drains a huge area of northeastern North America before emptying into the Mississippi. The French and British recognized its vital strategic and economic importance, and their competition for control of North America came to a head there in the middle of the eighteenth century. After Britain drove France from North America, the Shawnees faced British power head-on. A dozen years before American colonists rebelled against the British Empire, Shawnees participated in a multitribal war of independence. Colonial pressure on Indian lands continued unabated, however. Pioneers like Daniel Boone flooded into Kentucky, and Shawnee warriors fought them back as trespassers on their hunting lands. Kentucky became a bitterly contested "dark and bloody ground." The Ohio River became the major highway for settlers traveling west. The conquest of Kentucky and the Ohio Valley "was the first and greatest hurdle" for American national expansion. For almost twenty-five years, throughout the American Revolution and the years that followed, Shawnees fought to stop white settlement at the Ohio. Never again would Indians face Americans on such nearly equal terms as they did here; never again would Indians win victories of the magnitude they did here.[6] As the United States moved west, so did Shawnee resistance.

The Shawnees' defense of their own homeland merged into a broader defense of Indian country. Shawnees regularly allied with other Indian nations and time and again they took the lead in marshaling multitribal confederations. Always adamant about defending Shawnee land, Shawnee leaders became increasingly vocal advocates of the principle that, in a sense, the lands of every tribe belonged to all the tribes. That stance culminated in the first decade of the nineteenth century when two Shawnee brothers, Tenskwatawa, also known as the Shawnee Prophet, and the legendary war chief Tecumseh forged a multitribal coalition dedicated to the protection of all Indian lands and cultures.

As occasion demanded and opportunity offered, Shawnees also made common cause with the French and the British, although, in common with other inhabitants of the Ohio Valley, their larger goal was to prevent either European power from dominating the region. Time and again, European allies let them down and tribal alliances dissolved.

The death of Tecumseh and the collapse of his confederacy signaled the end of Shawnee military resistance and confirmed American dominance in lands they had fought to defend.

It was also, in a sense, the end of a war for America's heart and soul. The Ohio Valley that was key to European empire-building and American nation-building was also home to Indian nations whose cultural, economic, and societal values were often directly at odds with those of the invaders. The contest was not only about who should occupy the land, but about what kind of societies should exist there and what meanings the land would hold for them. From the moment they set foot on the continent, Europeans and then Americans depicted their conflicts with the Native peoples as an elemental battle between two ways of life, between, as they described it, civilization and savagery. The Shawnees no doubt saw it that way, too, although, had they used the terms, they would have had their own ideas about who was civilized and who was savage.

In histories and memories of the Old West, the Shawnees often featured as frontier terrorists. They burned cabins, killed and scalped settlers, routed American militia, and like the whites they fought, sometimes committed unspeakable atrocities. They were infamous for capturing Daniel Boone's daughter, and for capturing Daniel Boone himself on more than one occasion. Long after the fighting was over, pioneer families put children to bed with warnings that if they did not go to sleep the Shawnees would get them.[7] In their own minds, of course, Shawnees were freedom fighters, not terrorists. At a time when American patriots were urging colonists to unite against British imperialism, Shawnees urged Indians to unite against American expansion. They fought to keep the heartland of America free from aliens who threatened to steal the land and destroy the world. Thomas Ridout, an Englishman who was taken captive by the Shawnees in 1788, found that when he walked into Shawnee lodges, "The children would scream with terror, and cry out 'Shemanthe,' meaning Virginian, or the big knife."[8]

Euro-Americans who invaded Shawnee lands came from colonies and nation-states. They came from a society of government and laws, churches and Bibles, courts and jails, wealth and poverty, gentlemen and workers, masters and slaves. Men (and slaves), not women, did the farming. They valued individual ownership of property and individual success. Status was reflected in occupation, wealth, and clothing, and they were sure that Indians ranked below them in the order of things. Shawnee communities were based on clan and kinship; deference was paid to age, not to wealth or station; custom and public opinion, not laws and government, checked individual conduct. Women farmed, men hunted. Shawnees measured wealth in gifts given and in social capital rather than in money and material goods. They valued sharing and reciprocity as both an ideal and a practical way of living.

In Europe, people's ties to the land had undergone, and in some places were still undergoing, fundamental changes. In Britain, enclosures that had been occurring since the Middle Ages increased rapidly in the eighteenth century. Common grazing lands were divided up, and strips of arable land were consolidated into large fields, fenced and hedged, where improved methods of farming could be applied more efficiently. In the Highlands of Scotland, clan lands were being turned to large-estate sheep farming that brought higher rents and increased profits; clanspeople were being turned off the land. Uprooted from their homelands in Europe, colonists had no deep roots in America's land.

But tribal roots ran deep. Tribal homelands were hallowed ground held in common. As it was for other Native peoples, land was vital to their identity. Land was not just acreage, it was the total physical environment they inhabited: earth and sky, rivers and lakes, mountains and meadows. They drew both physical and spiritual sustenance from it, understood that human action could upset things, and maintained a relationship with the nonhuman inhabitants and forces in the physical environment. The ceremonies men and women performed kept things in balance and renewed the world; the stories they told preserved and revealed knowledge about it. Euro-Americans often described Indian country as chaotic, savage, and godless, but the Shawnee world had its own order, philosophy, and spirituality.[9]

In Europe, too, people had seen lands as repositories of history and identity, but with no historical attachment to land in America, colonists could only see it in terms of its economic potential.[10] Finding it in vast quantities, they treated it as a commodity: They measured it in acres and square miles, bounded it with markers, and bought and sold it for money. Shawnee leaders repeatedly insisted that God had given them their country and they had no right to sell it, let alone hand it over to strangers who would bound it and abuse it and build alien societies. The different philosophies are still in conflict: Native attempts to preserve and protect sites they hold sacred clash with "America's values of inviolable property and the government's mandate to keep its public lands available" to campers, tourists, sportsmen, and lumbermen.[11]

Shawnee households had rights to fields and individual women owned crops, but the fields were grouped together and planted collectively.[12] Jonathan Alder, who was taken captive when he was nine years old, lived for thirteen years with the Shawnees but left them in 1795. Much had changed: His adoptive parents had died, his marriage to a Shawnee woman did not work out, and white settlers were arriving in growing numbers. "Finally," recalled Alder, "I came to the conclusion that I would rather live with the white people and own property the way you could not do to any extent with the Indians."[13]

The two worldviews collided head-on in Kentucky and the Ohio country. Shawnees fought to preserve their homelands and hunting territories; Americans fought to transform them into fields and pastures, with fences that penned in domesticated animals and marked property boundaries. Pioneers who hunted in the same forests as the Shawnees observed a different hunting ethic and had different relations with the animals. In the Shawnee world, humans and animals communicated, hunters dreamed the whereabouts of their prey and offered prayers to the spirits of the animals that gave their bodies so that the people might live. Humans might even shift form into animals. Shawnees saw spiritual forces in all parts of their world. Proper rituals were necessary to harvest plant and animal life and keep the world in balance. White invaders ignored hunting rituals, slaughtered game wastefully, felled trees with fire and axes, tried to hold the land they seized as private property, and seemed to hoard wealth for its own sake. Shawnees must have thought they were *motchitteheckie*, ill-disposed, evil-minded people, or just *wannine*, crazy. They said as much, complaining at the beginning of the American Revolution that the whites were "coming in the middle of us like crazy people and want to shove us off our land entirely."[14]

Shawnee hunters read the woods in ways few Euro-

Americans could. The forests that Europeans described as a menacing and "trackless wilderness" were alive with meaning for Shawnees. They observed signs of animal and human activity, and they left signs for others, placing rocks and twigs in particular positions, etching messages in trees, marking trails, and imparting information. In an environment inhabited by the spirits of animals and ancestors, Indians traveled with a light foot, halting at ritual stopping places to make offerings of tobacco or food and avoiding other places associated with misfortune or evil spirits. Animals and birds could be messengers and omens. Rattlesnakes were "grandfathers" to be revered and placated with an offering of tobacco, not venomous reptiles to be killed out of hand.[15]

Some Euro-Americans learned to read the woods this way, but most dismissed such Native knowledge as "primitive superstitions." Eighteenth-century Enlightenment thinking held that human societies developed by stages: "savage" (hunting and fishing), "barbarian" (herding), a first phase of "civilized" based on agriculture, and "fully civilized" based on commerce and manufacturing. Indians were regarded as people at a lower stage of development who had little or nothing to teach Europeans. Indians could learn to live like civilized people, but they must be shown the way. Euro-Americans tried to convert them to their way of life, to make them see the world as they saw it. They sent missionaries into Indian communities, brought Indian youths to colonial colleges, and imposed farming programs in Indian villages. For men like Thomas Jefferson, the plan was not to exterminate each and every Indian; it was to change them forever so they ceased to exist as Indians. Consequently, a contest of cultures accompanied the struggle for land. Efforts to "civilize" Indians usually took second place to taking their land, and the two goals were often in tension. But not always, and Shawnees realized it: American expansion meant taking their land; American "civilization" and Christianity meant severing their spiritual connection to the land.

At a time when Euro-Americans were experiencing massive transformations in their own world, Shawnees fought to prevent the newcomers from imposing wrenching changes in *their* world. When that proved impossible, they fought to limit the impacts, channel the directions, and give their own meaning to the changes. They tried to stave off cultural assaults and to remain separate, even as they chose to adopt some pieces and practices from the new culture.

At the same time, they converted some Euro-Americans into Indians. Some whites found life in Indian communities an attractive alternative to life in frontier settlements. Captives were often adopted into Shawnee families and transformed into Shawnees themselves. Sometimes they preferred not to return home, a phenomenon that thinking men like Benjamin Franklin found deeply troubling in its implications for white society's assumed superiority. Franklin said Europeans who had lived in Indian societies soon "become disgusted with our manner of life." Hector St. John de Crèvecoeur thought Indian society exerted an "imperceptible charm" on white people. There must be, he said, something in their social bond "singularly captivating and far superior to anything to be boasted of among us."[16]

It would be wrong to depict the frontier as a clear boundary separating Indian and white worlds and moving steadily westward. Frontiers are zones of interaction as well as separation, sponges soaking up influences as much as barriers to communication. When Indians and Europeans met, both were affected, although not necessarily to the same degree. David Jones's account of Shawnee resistance to his religious message also reveals much about the meeting of cultures on the frontiers. Although the British and Americans regularly tried to run boundary lines that ate up Indian lands, and Indians fought to halt white expansion at the Appalachian Mountains or the Ohio River, the cultural conflict was not always clearly delineated. White people sometimes lived in Indian villages, Indians and whites often intermarried, and they regularly borrowed from each other's technology and culture. At Chillicothe, Jones lodged with Moses Henry, a trader and gunsmith from Lancaster, Pennsylvania, who had lived for several years in the town, married to a white woman who had been taken captive as a girl, adopted into the tribe, and now spoke the language as well as any Shawnee. About twenty other white people lived in the town. Three miles northwest of Chillicothe lived Captain Alexander McKee of the British Indian department, the son of a Pennsylvania trader and a Shawnee mother. McKee had a Shawnee wife and family. Moses Henry, who brought the Shawnees guns and was content to live among them, was accepted; David Jones, who brought Christianity and was determined to change them, was not. The Shawnees did not blindly reject everything white men had to offer; they were selective in what they acquired or accepted. They fought to make those choices on their own terms.

On the frontiers, Europeans and Indians alike grew corn, hunted white-tailed deer, ate similar foods, paddled canoes, wore moccasins and hunting shirts, killed with guns and tomahawks, took scalps, lived in bark or log lodgings, and rode horses the Spaniards had brought to America two centuries earlier. Missionary David McClure said backcountry Virginians were "generally white Savages, and subsist by hunting, and live like the Indians." Some whites married Indian women. Blue Jacket, a stalwart defender of Shawnee land and independence, had a French-Shawnee wife, owned livestock, visited Philadelphia, and sent his son to be educated in Detroit. Daniel Boone the Indian fighter rubbed shoulders with Shawnees, and Shawnee influences rubbed off on him and on others.[17] Indians often said that God made wild animals for them and tame animals for whites, and they resisted the invasion of cattle, pigs, and sheep, but in time Shawnees, too, began to own livestock.[18] The gulf separating the Shawnees from the people who invaded their land was not an impassable chasm. There was much that brought Indians and Europeans together, and there were many who attempted to reach across the cultural gulf to fashion new relationships. Travelers from the East often said they saw little difference between backcountry settlers and Indians. Indians and Europeans entered into trade, alliances, and other arrangements of mutual interest based on shared understandings. But the escalating competition for land submerged common humanity in a sea of antagonisms. The line dividing Indians and whites drew increasingly tight, and became increasingly contested and racial, leaving little room for men like Blue Jacket and Daniel Boone and little opportunity for new kinds of societies to grow from the confluence of cultures.[19]

Remarkable as the Shawnees were in their resistance, this book does not try to idealize or romanticize them. No genetic mandate or tribal master plan dictated that all Shawnees oppose the Americans and their ways all the time. Shawnees debated issues of peace and war, and even how to fight their battles, and divided over the paths they should follow. Not all Shawnees insisted on standing and fighting. Retreat could be an effective strategy of cultural resistance against the imposition and influence of Euro-American ways as well as a necessary step to move people out of harm's way. Many preferred

migration to endless confrontation. What British Indian superintendent Sir William Johnson said about Indians generally applied particularly to the Shawnees: They would never
accept subjection to a foreign power "whilst they have any
men, or an open country to retire to."[20] Often they moved only
to take up the fight again in a new location.

Like any people, Shawnees sometimes changed their
minds as circumstances changed, and individuals sometimes
made decisions for their own interests rather than the good of
the whole. People wavered, disagreed, displayed human
weakness, and grew weary of the fight. Some found opportunities for survival in adaptation rather than outright resistance, and some sought opportunities for personal gain even
as they fought on. Many chose day-to-day survival over heroic
resistance. By the time Tecumseh issued his call for Indian
unity, the majority of Shawnees had already retreated across
the Mississippi, and most of those who remained in Ohio
turned a deaf ear to him. Nevertheless, in the vast colonial
collision that constitutes so much of American history, the
Shawnees stand out as hardliners when it came to defending
Native lands, Native rights, and Native ways of life.

I have been encountering Shawnees in documents from
the eighteenth and nineteenth centuries for more than thirty
years, ever since I began reading through British Indian department manuscripts in the British Museum and the Public
Records Office in London. Even in those records, written by

alien people, the Shawnees emerge as remarkable people battling massive historical change, and people who knew what they were fighting for. I do not pretend or presume to relate the Shawnees' own history. I have no particular expertise or cultural experience to do such a thing, and no tribal insights to share. Other authors, Shawnee people, can provide more culturally grounded books that draw on tribal stories, traditions, and memories.[21] This short book simply relates a crucial piece of American history and places the Shawnees center stage. Indians are supposed to be silent in the records written by history's winners, but Shawnees speak from the records kept by the British, French, Spaniards, and Americans. Shawnee orators explained that for them the struggle for America was not only a contest for resources but also a clash between two ways of life and between two different worldviews. They fought for a different vision of America.

THE SHAWNEES
AND THE
WAR FOR AMERICA

1

THE GREATEST TRAVELERS
IN AMERICA

IN THE SPRING of 1805, a one-eyed Shawnee notorious for his loud mouth and his hard drinking fell into a trance. He awoke to report that he had experienced a visionary journey to the Master of Life, who gave him a message of salvation for his people: Indians must renounce the white man's influences and return to traditional ways of living. Formerly known as Lalawethika, he took a new name, Tenskwatawa, meaning the Open Door. Whites came to know him as the Shawnee Prophet. His teachings struck a chord with many Indian peoples who had suffered military defeat, land loss, and cultural assault. He offered a voice to oppressed people, an explanation for a world turned upside down, and a recipe for self-redemption. If Indians returned to living healthy and moral lives, the Master of Life would look favorably on them again and drive out their white oppressors. Followers flocked to hear his message.

His brother, Tecumseh, extended this movement of spiritual rejuvenation into a struggle for independence. He appealed to freedom fighters of all nations to set aside tribal interests and join him in a confederacy of warriors devoted to defending Indian country against American expansion. Messengers fanned out across Indian country and Tecumseh himself traveled far and wide. Warriors from as many as thirty tribes rallied to the cause.

Tecumseh was a remarkable individual by any standards, but his ability to attract followers throughout the eastern woodlands depended on more than his charisma and fiery oratory. He was a Shawnee. No Indian people had moved so often, traveled so widely, or knew better how the invaders had eroded Indian country and repeatedly pushed Indian people westward. No one could speak with more authority about the need for Indian peoples to unite in a final confrontation with the invaders who were destroying their world.

In 1754, Britain and France were on the brink of war in North America. The British Board of Trade, recognizing that England needed to do more to win the Indians to its side, turned for advice to Edmund Atkin, a member of the South Carolina Council and a prominent Charleston merchant with plenty of experience in the Indian trade. Atkin responded with a long letter in which he detailed the importance of the

Indians in the imperial struggle for America, the respective policies of Britain and France in dealing with the tribes, the role of the Indian trade, and the "character and disposition of the various Indian nations," particularly those in the South. He also submitted a plan for overhauling the British system of managing Indian affairs. Up until this time, the various colonial governments had conducted their own dealings with the tribes. Atkin favored centralizing Indian affairs under two imperial superintendents, one for the North and another for the South. The Board of Trade agreed and appointed Atkin southern superintendent in 1756. The Shawnees received little coverage in Atkin's review of Indian country, dwarfed by the attention given to more numerous and powerful nations like the Cherokees and Choctaws. But he described Shawnee movements that took them into what are now the states of New York, Pennsylvania, Ohio, South Carolina, Georgia, and Alabama. And he pronounced them "Stout, Bold, Cunning and the greatest Travellers in America."[1] It was a fitting description for a people whose history consisted of large doses of movement and conflict. They waged their struggles to remain Shawnee across several centuries and across much of America.

The Shawnees seem to have originated in the Ohio Valley, a region inhabited by Native people for at least ten thousand years before Europeans arrived. Archaeologists, trying to reconstruct a picture of Indian life from traces left in the ground, identify the cultures and phases as Early Woodland or Adena (500 B.C. to roughly A.D. 100), Middle Woodland or Hopewell (about 100 B.C. to A.D. 500), and Late Woodland— the thousand years or so before contact with Europeans. The ancient inhabitants left the Ohio Valley pockmarked with earthen mounds constructed for burial and other ceremonial purposes. They were great traders, exchanging goods through networks extending across vast distances.

The Shawnees may have descended, at least in part, from a Late Woodland people known to archaeologists as the Fort Ancient Culture, although not all scholars agree. The Fort Ancient people lived from about 1400 to 1650 in an area that embraced southern Ohio, southern Indiana, western Virginia, and northern Kentucky. They occupied riverbank villages composed of rows of lodgings, as well as larger structures that may have been antecedents of the council houses later erected by Shawnees. Using digging sticks and hoes made of stone or shell with wooden handles, Fort Ancient women grew corn, beans, squash, and sunflowers. The men hunted elk and other game with bows and arrows and fished with hooks and nets. Fort Ancient people also made unpainted pottery and ornaments of bone and shell.

The people who emerged into history as the Shaw-nees were members of the Algonquian language family. They were culturally and linguistically related to other Algonquian-speaking peoples like the Delawares, Miamis,

Kickapoos, Illinois, and Sauks and Foxes, although not necessarily allied with them. In intertribal diplomacy, Shawnees addressed the Delawares as grandfathers, the Wyandots and Iroquois as uncles or elder brothers, and other tribes as younger brothers.[2]

The Shawnees traditionally comprised five divisions, though it is not certain whether these divisions originally constituted different tribes, which came together to form the Shawnees, or if they developed during their migrations. Each division came to have specific responsibilities. The Chillicothe and Thawekila divisions took care of political concerns affecting the whole tribe and generally supplied tribal political leaders; the Mekoches were concerned with health and medicine and provided healers and counselors; the Pekowis were responsible for matters of religion and ritual; and the Kispokos generally took the lead in preparing and training for war and supplying war chiefs. These divisions seem to have functioned as semiautonomous political units, each with its own chief. They occupied particular towns (often named after the division), possessed their own sacred bundles, and sometimes conducted their own foreign policies with other tribes. In addition to the five divisions, Shawnee society was composed of clans. According to information provided by the Shawnee Prophet in the nineteenth century, there were originally as many as thirty-four clans, but only a dozen remained by his day: the Snake, Turtle, Raccoon, Turkey, Hawk, Deer, Bear,

Wolf, Panther, Elk, Buffalo, and Tree clans. Shawnees inherited their divisional and clan membership from their fathers.[3]

Like many other Native peoples of the Northeast and Midwest, Shawnees believed that North America was an island in a vast body of water. A giant sea turtle, "placed there for that purpose by the Great Spirit," supported it. Waashaa Monetoo, the Great Spirit, recreated the world after a great flood and the Shawnees were the first people he introduced to it. They were a chosen people. The Shawnee Prophet said: "When the Shawnees first crossed the sea, the Great Spirit told them to go to Shawnee river, which was the centre of this Island. That the earth had not yet a heart as all men and animals had & that he would put them, the Shawnees, at Shawnee river for the heart of the Earth." From there he told them they would go to the Mad River and then to the Mississippi, "where they would remain a short time and where they would discover something coming towards them (the whites), which would make them very poor and miserable." The Shawnee chief Black Hoof said the Great Spirit gave the Shawnees "a piece of his own heart." They would need it.[4]

When the French Jesuit missionary Jacques Marquette traveled down the Mississippi River in 1673, he passed the mouth of the Wabash-Ohio River. His Indian guides told him that its waters flowed from the east, "where dwell the people called Chaouanons [Shawnees] in so great numbers that in one district there are as many as 23 villages, and fifteen in

another quite near one another." French maps in the late seventeenth century located the Chaouanons on the Ohio and
Cumberland Rivers, and some label the Cumberland as the
"rivière des Chaouanons." From their Ohio and Cumberland
Valley villages, the Shawnees appear to have traveled widely.
They participated in far-reaching exchange networks that
funneled European goods through Indian country, and some
likely traded directly with the Spaniards in Florida. Illinois
Indians told Marquette that Shawnees came to their villages
"laden with glass beads."[5]

The Ohio Valley was a dangerous place in the late seventeenth century. The ripple effects of the European invasion of
North America affected and destroyed lives far from the
scenes of the first face-to-face encounters. Europeans brought
with them many diseases to which Native Americans had
had no previous exposure and against which, consequently,
they lacked immunity. Smallpox, measles, influenza, plague,
and a host of other killer diseases took a devastating toll on
Indian populations. Mortality rates in excess of 75 percent
were not uncommon. Direct evidence is lacking, but European germs racing along trade and communication networks
likely killed Indians in the Ohio Valley who had not laid eyes
on European people.

The inhabitants of the Ohio also felt the impact of European trade and technology. When Europeans and Indians
met, they naturally exchanged things they had for things they

wanted: Europeans wanted the beaver pelts and deerskins that Indian hunters could provide; Indians wanted the woolen blankets, metal pots, steel axes, and firearms produced in European mills and factories. European colonists depended heavily on trade with Indians for food and prosperity, and many major cities—Quebec, Albany, New York, Detroit, Charleston, St. Louis—began life as trading posts. Indian people readily adopted trade items that made their lives easier. Unfortunately, trade with Europeans came at a heavy cost and had lethal consequences. It accelerated the spread of new diseases, introduced alcohol into Indian communities, increased the slaughter of wildlife, and sparked an arms race in Indian country. Seventeenth-century muskets were cumbersome and unreliable—in many circumstances they were no match for the speed, velocity, and accuracy of bows and arrows in expert Indian hands—but guns had formidable killing power, and Indian warriors were eager to have them.

When the French penetrated North America via the St. Lawrence River at the beginning of the seventeenth century, they established alliances with Indian peoples in eastern Canada and around the Great Lakes. In 1609, Samuel de Champlain, the founder of Quebec, joined some of his allies in a skirmish against their Mohawk enemies on the shores of Lake Champlain, near where Fort Ticonderoga in New York stands today. It was a small affair as battles go: The Indians lined up, shouting insults and invoking their war medicine.

Protected by shields and body armor fashioned from wood and leather, they made ready to do battle with spears and arrows. Champlain and his French comrades stepped forward with their muskets, shot down several Mohawk chiefs, and put the rest to flight. The fight was over in a matter of minutes, but its repercussions reverberated across northeastern America for years.

Indian warriors needed guns to compete against armed enemies, and they needed beaver pelts to buy guns. As French missionaries and traders pushed west into Indian country, Ottawa and Huron traders from the Great Lakes paddled their canoes down to Montreal and Quebec, eager to trade pelts for guns and metal weapons that, literally, gave them an edge over their enemies. The Mohawks, who together with the Oneidas, Cayugas, Onondagas, and Senecas, made up the League of the Iroquois stretching the length of upstate New York, had to look elsewhere for guns and ammunition. In the 1620s they pushed aside the Mahicans so they could trade directly with the Dutch on the Hudson River, near what became Albany, New York. After the English defeated the Dutch and took possession of New York in the 1660s, the Mohawks dealt with the British. Indian hunters killed beaver in unprecedented numbers for European markets that seemed insatiable. Beaver were less plentiful in Iroquois country than in the northern forests of their rivals, and as they depleted their own supplies of beaver, the Iroquois feared they would fall behind in the arms race. They began to raid traders from other tribes heading down to Montreal with fur-laden canoes and extended their raids into other peoples' territories. Violence escalated. Iroquois warriors who fell in combat, as well as people who died from the new diseases, had to be avenged. Iroquois warriors traditionally conducted raids that brought home captives they might ritually torture or adopt into their clans and communities to replace deceased relatives, with clan mothers often deciding the fate of the captives. The new kinds of warfare intensified the need to wage old ways of warfare.

The deadly cycle of furs and guns, war and revenge spread devastation across large swaths of America. In 1648–49, Iroquois war parties shattered the once-powerful and prosperous confederacy of the Wendat or Huron people who lived in the Georgian Bay region of Lake Huron. They killed French missionaries, destroyed Huron villages, killed hundreds of people, and adopted hundreds more. Survivors fled in all directions; some moved eventually to northwestern Ohio, where they became known as Wyandots. Iroquois raiding parties struck into New England, the Susquehanna Valley, and the Ohio country. Many peoples fled from Ohio to the western Great Lakes to escape the onslaught. Outgunned and outnumbered, the Shawnees scattered.[6]

In 1683, several hundred Shawnees arrived at Fort St. Louis, a post Robert Cavelier de La Salle had built at Starved Rock on the Illinois River. Others migrated to the Southeast and took up residence on the Savannah River in Georgia. Shawnees from the Cumberland may have traveled to South Carolina earlier, passing through the Cumberland Gap and traveling down the Great Warriors Path, which led from the Ohio River through Kentucky, into Cherokee country and the Southeast. The name "Shawnee" means "southerner" in some tribal languages. Substantial numbers of Shawnees appeared in South Carolina by 1680, and the South Carolinians welcomed them as a buffer to protect their settlements against local Westo and other Indians. The Shawnees displaced the Westos and raided them for captives whom they sold as slaves to the Carolinians for guns. They also fought against the Catawbas and clashed with other slave-trading nations like the Chickasaws. Shawnees also settled in western Virginia, where they occupied several villages before 1700. In the eighteenth century, Shawnees had settlements on the Tallapoosa River in Alabama, where they lived alongside the Creek Indians. One group took refuge there following the Yamassee War in South Carolina in 1715, and others gravitated to the area, establishing a long-standing connection between Shawnees and Creeks. Shawnees from Ohio continued to raid, trade, and visit with southern Indians throughout the century.

Shawnees also began moving to Pennsylvania.[7] They established a large village on the Delaware River in the 1690s and built other villages along the Susquehanna. Some moved from the Savannah River to Pennsylvania in 1707, to escape increasing hostilities with Carolina; another band followed after the Yamassee War. Still more arrived from Illinois, Ohio, and the Carolinas in the eighteenth century.

The Shawnees enjoyed good relations with William Penn, who, as governor of Pennsylvania, tried to ensure fair dealings with the Indians in trade and land transactions. But things were never the same after Penn died in 1717, and as relations with English traders and settlers deteriorated, Shawnees began to move west across the Allegheny Mountains. When the Pennsylvania authorities heard that Shawnees had visited the French governor in Montreal, they feared the French were trying to win them over. The governor of Pennsylvania requested a meeting in Philadelphia with Shawnee delegates in the fall of 1732 and asked them why they had moved and what they were up to communicating with the French. He reminded them of the alliance they had entered into with the English in Pennsylvania and asked them to return. The Shawnees replied that "the place where they are now Settled Suits them much better than to live nearer," and "that they can live much better there than they possibly can any where on Sasquehannah."[8]

Migrating served several purposes for the Shawnees. It was a way to escape the influence of the Iroquois, who, when dealing with the British, claimed to speak for and dominate the Shawnees, Delawares, and other tribes on the basis of having "conquered" them in the seventeenth century. It was also a way to move away from the abuses of rum traders who got Indians drunk and swindled them out of their furs. Shawnee leaders protested, and on occasion even staved in kegs of rum in their villages, but Pennsylvania failed to pass legislation with any teeth. After much negotiation, a delegation of twenty-one Shawnees came to Philadelphia in 1739, agreed to a treaty that reaffirmed their original treaty with William Penn in 1701, and promised not to join any nation that was hostile to Great Britain. Pennsylvania continued to ask for assurances of Shawnee loyalty and Shawnee diplomats continued to give them, but the Shawnees were moving out from under Pennsylvania's influence and continued to talk with the French.[9]

Shawnees moved so often and dispersed so widely that they sometimes seemed like a people without a homeland of their own. By the second half of the eighteenth century, however, although some Shawnee bands remained in Virginia, Alabama, and Kentucky, the Ohio Valley was once again the core of Shawnee life and culture. Shawnee migrants established a major village on the Ohio, near the mouth of the Scioto River. It became known as Lower Shawnee Town. Surveyor Christopher Gist, who was in the Ohio Valley in 1750–51, described it as a community of 300 men, indicating a total population of about 1,200 (unless by "men" he meant warriors, in which case 1,500 would be a more likely figure). The town comprised 140 houses on both sides of the Ohio

River. In the center of the town stood a bark-covered council house about ninety feet long.[10] Lower Shawnee Town was a key center in dealings with other tribes and with Europeans before it was abandoned in 1758, at which point most of the inhabitants established the town of Chillicothe farther up the Scioto. Other Shawnee bands settled on lands in Ohio set aside for them by the Wyandots, just as Shawnees had previously settled on lands provided by Creeks and Delawares.

Even so, Ohio was not an exclusively Shawnee homeland. Other peoples were moving into Ohio in the first half of the eighteenth century. Delawares and Mingos—primarily Senecas and some Cayugas who moved west—also took up residence there. Miamis and other Indians from farther west were drawn to the area by the increasing presence of European traders.[11]

Like their neighbors, the Shawnees inhabited semipermanent villages, moved with the seasons, and practiced a mixed economy. Women planted corn, beans, and squash in the spring and harvested the crops in the fall. They held Bread Dances in the spring and fall, to ask and give thanks for a bountiful harvest and hunting season. For several days in August they marked the first harvest with a Green Corn Ceremony, probably adopted from the Creeks. Women supplemented the diet by gathering herbs, roots, berries, and various wild plants and nuts. After the crops were gathered in, families dispersed to hunt. They often crossed the Ohio

River for extended hunting trips, sometimes two or three months long, in Kentucky. The men hunted deer, elk, bears, turkeys, and buffalo. In the winter, when the animals' pelts were thickest, they hunted for the fur trade. During late winter and early spring, people reassembled in the villages, tapped the sap from maple trees, and boiled it into sugar. The men assisted in clearing the fields for planting, and the annual cycle began again.

Shawnee social structure was loose and flexible, revolving around kinship and bands. It was a society that could accommodate movement, separation, and reassembling without falling apart. Likewise, Shawnee dwellings were easily dismantled and rebuilt, as suited a people who moved regularly. Family wigwams were constructed of wooden poles covered with sheets of bark. Thomas Wildcat Alford, a nineteenth-century Shawnee, said a dexterous Shawnee woman could build one "easily and quickly."[12] The council houses built in the larger towns for political and ceremonial functions were much more substantial. Shaker missionaries described one they visited in 1807 as an "immense building," 150 feet long and 34 feet wide, raised on rows of large hewed posts and with four doors.[13]

Political authority was limited and diffused: Chiefs seem to have been hereditary, but they led by reputation and example, not by rank or office. Like most eastern woodlands tribes, the Shawnees had civil or peace chiefs and war chiefs.

Civil chiefs tended to be mature men who had earned a reputation for good sense and whose counsel guided the people during times of peace and in everyday affairs. In times of war, civil chiefs temporarily handed authority to younger men who had attained a following because of their military prowess and who led war parties out from the villages. On returning to the village, or when peace returned, the war chiefs handed authority back to the civil chiefs. Tribal councils of elderly men also debated and decided important matters. Women as well as men had war and civil chiefs. The Shawnee Prophet said the principal duty of the female peace chief was to prevent unnecessary bloodshed: She would exert her influence to restrain the war chiefs and ensure that conflict occurred only as a last resort. The female chiefs also had oversight of women's affairs in the village, such as directing the planting and the arrangement of feasts.[14] A Quaker who was surprised to see an old woman speaking in an Indian council near the Susquehanna River in 1706 and asked his interpreter why was told "that some women were wiser than some men, and that they had not done anything for many years without the council of this ancient, grave woman."[15] Increasing contact with Europeans disrupted the balance of influences that had traditionally worked to keep war in its place: White men ignored women when dealing with Indian allies, and escalating conflicts gave war chiefs greater clout in Indian communities.

Whether in war or peace, Shawnee chiefs exercised only limited authority. Their influence depended upon their individual character, their continued effectiveness, and the willingness of people to listen to their counsel or follow them into battle. They had no means of enforcing their will. The Reverend David Jones said Shawnees were "strangers to civil power and authority." They believed that God made them free and "that one man has no natural right to rule over another." And—several years before Thomas Jefferson inscribed his self-evident truths in the Declaration of Independence—Jones noted: "In this point they agree with our greatest politicians, who affirm that a ruler's authority extends no further than the pleasure of the people, and when any exceeds that power given, it may be justly asked, by what authority doest thou these things, and who gave thee that authority?"[16]

Despite their loose political systems, Shawnees proved to be astute politicians and adept international diplomats. By the time they reassembled in the Ohio Valley, they had experiences and connections linking them to Indian peoples over much of the eastern woodlands. They were positioned to function as the hub of tribal networks reaching from the Great Lakes to the Gulf of Mexico, and from the Alleghenies to the Mississippi. Shawnee emissaries carrying wampum belts ran woodland trails and Shawnee council houses hummed with a babel of languages when they convened multitribal congresses.[17] Shawnee villages commonly accommodated outsiders—

traders, Indian agents, spouses, visitors—and beyond the villages Shawnees regularly encountered Indian peoples from many other nations, Pennsylvanians, Virginians and Carolinians, Frenchmen, Spaniards, and British.

The Shawnees earned a reputation as fierce warriors, among Indians and whites alike. Colonel Charles Stuart, who fought against them at the Battle of Point Pleasant in 1774, reckoned they were "the most bloody and terrible" of all Indians, "holding all other men as well Indians as whites, in contempt as warriors, in comparison with themselves." They evidently boasted they had killed ten times more white people than any other tribe. They were "a well-formed, active, and ingenious people," said Stuart; "assuming and imperious in the presence of others not of their own nation, and sometimes very cruel."[18]

Of course, they were not just warriors. John Norton, an adopted Mohawk of Scots-Cherokee parentage, who knew many Shawnees in the early nineteenth century, said they varied greatly in individual character but were "generally open and frank,—their affability, good humour, and Vivacity render them agreeable to Strangers,—and they always seem to derive pleasure from the practice of Hospitality, & in doing all in their power to make agreeable the sojourn of those who visit their Villages." They were "great Talkers, and their Language is very melodious and strong, well adapted to beautify and embellish the flowerings of natural eloquence." They had "a Countenance strongly expressive of energy, good nature, and Vivacity." Even the Reverend David Jones, who received a cold reception when he tried to peddle his religion in Chillicothe, had to admit: "They are the most cheerful and merry people that I ever saw . . . both men and women in laughing exceed any nation that ever came under my notice."[19]

Observers described Shawnees as mostly tall, well-built, but slender.[20] Jones, for all his prejudices, provided some useful information on Shawnee society and left a pen-picture of how Shawnee people looked in the late eighteenth century, by which time European trade items were a part of their world:

> The men wear shirts, match-coats, breech-clouts, leggings and mockesons, called by them *mockeetha*. Their ornaments are silver plates about their arms, above and below their elbows. Nose jewels are common. They paint their faces, and cut the rim of their ears, so as to stretch them very large. Their head is dressed in the best mode, with a black silk handkerchief about it; or else the head is all shaved only the crown, which is left for the scalp. The hair in it has a swan's plume, or some trinket of silver tied in it. The women wear short shifts over their stroud, which serves for a petticoat. Some times a calico bed-gown. Their hair is parted and tied behind. They paint only in spots in common on their cheeks. Their ears are

never cut, but some have ten silver rings in them. One squaa will have near five hundred silver broaches stuck in her shift, stroud and leggings. Men and women are very proud, but men seem to exceed in this vice."[21]

Oliver Spencer, a white captive who lived with the Shawnees in the early 1790s, described the dress of Shawnee women as consisting of a calico shirt extending about six inches below the waist, a skirt or petticoat reaching just below the knee, a pair of leggings, and moccasins. Women of all ages wore basically the same outfit but whereas older women donned plain and simple clothes, young and middle-aged women favored finery. "Young belles" had "the tops of their moccasins curiously wrought with beads, ribbons, and porcupine quills; the borders of their leggings and the bottom and edges of their strouds [a kind of cloth manufactured in England] tastily bound with ribbons, edged with beads of various colors; and frequently on their moccasins and leggings small tufts of deer's hair, dyed red and confined in small pieces of tin, rattling as they walked." They covered their shirts with silver brooches of various sizes and wore silver bracelets and armbands.[22] Shawnees were rumored to have silver mines in their country and American militia raiding Shawnee villages hoped to carry off silver as well as scalps, horses, and other plunder. There would be many such raids across the Ohio in the late eighteenth century.

The Shawnee bands that reassembled in the Ohio Valley by the middle of the century were coming home, returning to their ancient roots in the area. They had traveled, traded, and fought across large stretches of North America, and they brought with them experiences, knowledge, influences, and individuals acquired along the way. They were well equipped to play a leading role in the multicultural Indian world that developed in Ohio, and to take the lead in marshaling a broader Indian defense of that world. But as it had in the seventeenth century, war in the late eighteenth century again produced migration and division among the Shawnees. In the years following the American Revolution, most Shawnees migrated west of the Mississippi; more followed after the Indian Removal Act of 1830. By the early nineteenth century, Shawnee groups lived in what is now Ohio, Indiana, Ontario, Missouri, and Texas, before most came together again, first at a reservation in Kansas and then in Oklahoma. Historic Shawnee village sites have been identified in at least sixteen different states, and as far apart as Maryland and Mexico.[23] A hundred years after Atkin wrote, Shawnees were still among the greatest travelers in America.

2

TAKING ON THE BRITISH EMPIRE

IN RETURNING TO the Ohio Valley, the Shawnees put themselves at the focal point of a contest between the superpowers of eighteenth-century Europe. Britain and France each believed that whoever controlled the Ohio country would control North America. The forks of the Ohio, where the Ohio, Allegheny, and Monongahela Rivers meet, formed the gateway to the West. France claimed the Ohio country on the basis of discoveries made in the late seventeenth century. The British claimed it on the basis of colonial charters that granted land as far west as the Pacific Ocean. They also claimed that the Iroquois were British subjects who in turn claimed the Ohio country by right of conquest in the seventeenth century. The Iroquois presumed to act as spokesmen for western Indians in dealing with the British and also became astute at playing off the French and the various English colonies against each other. Britain and France each tried to assert its power in the Ohio country through Indian allies, and through trade. The Indian peoples who lived there wanted European trade but also wanted to preserve their own independence from the British, the French, and the Iroquois. They, too, played off the rival parties—they sometimes flew French and British flags simultaneously over their lodges. A storm of contests and quarrels was brewing between European powers, English colonies, private traders, various tribes, and factions within tribes. The Shawnees had come home to a battlefield.[1]

Eventually, Shawnees sided with the French in the conflict, but at first they watched uneasily as outsiders jostled for position in the Ohio Valley. At the Treaty of Lancaster, Pennsylvania, in 1744, the Iroquois ceded land between the Susquehanna River and the Allegheny Mountains, as well as their remaining claims to land within the boundaries of Virginia and Maryland. Virginia's colonial charter placed its western boundary at the Pacific. In the colonists' eyes, the Iroquois had relinquished their claims to the Ohio country and it was open for trade and settlement.[2] Speculators formed the Ohio Company of Virginia to sell lands at the confluence of the Allegheny and Monongahela Rivers. Between September 1750 and March 1752, the company dispatched Christopher Gist on two journeys to survey lands as far down as the falls of the Ohio. The Indians knew what he was up to. They asked him where their land was supposed to be, since "the French claimed all the Land on one Side the River Ohio & the English on the other Side."[3]

Shawnee alliance with the French was by no means a foregone conclusion. Traders from Pennsylvania and Virginia pushed into the Ohio country, following the westward-moving Shawnees and Delawares and offering the Indians goods of a quality and price the French could not match. The French pressured the Indians to expel them. The Shawnees saw no reason to do so and the French tried to bully them. They picked the wrong people. In 1749, Captain Pierre Joseph Céleron de Blainville, former commandant at Detroit, led an expedition from Montreal through the upper Ohio Valley, a show of force intended to impress the Indians with French power. En route, he buried lead plates claiming the region for Louis XV. The locals were not impressed: An old Shawnee chief, Kakowatchiky, who was bedridden and blind, apparently said, "Shoot him." The Shawnees did not shoot Céleron, but they were clearly not intimidated.[4] In 1750, a force of Frenchmen and Indians from the north attacked a Shawnee village, killing a warrior and taking three captives. The Shawnees pursued the raiders and captured five Frenchmen and several Indians. Instead of bowing to French pressure, the Shawnees sent a message to the governor of Pennsylvania declaring they would "not suffer ourselves to be insulted any more." They asked the English to support them in striking the French and show "that you don't speak for nothing."[5]

But the British failed to take advantage of the opportunity, and the French reasserted their presence. In 1752, Charles Langlade, son of an Ottawa woman and a French trader, led a war party of 250 Ottawas and Ojibwas in a surprise attack and destroyed a Miami village at Pickawillany in Ohio that had become a center for trading with the English. The next year, the French began building a string of forts stretching from Lake Erie to the Forks of the Ohio. In 1754, they constructed Fort Duquesne at the Forks of the Ohio, the site of modern-day Pittsburgh.

French forts in the West threatened to stifle English colonies in the East. The governor of Virginia sent a young lieutenant, George Washington, into the Ohio Valley to demand that the French withdraw—a rather futile gesture—and then again to force their withdrawal. After a messy affair in which Washington's men and their Indian allies killed a dozen French soldiers—murdered them, the French claimed—Washington surrendered to a superior French force and was sent packing to Virginia. In 1755, Britain dispatched a professional army to get the job done. General Edward Braddock's army of British regulars and colonial militia hacked a road through the forests and across the mountains and came within striking distance of Fort Duquesne. But Braddock alienated the Indians by his haughty attitude and his ill-judged declaration that if Britain won, "No Savage should inherit the land." Determined that they should indeed inherit the land, the Shawnees and other Ohio Indians abandoned Braddock. Some went over to the French, joining Indians from the Great Lakes.

When Braddock's men crossed the Monongahela River, the French dispatched a sortie, composed primarily of Indians, from Fort Duquesne. When the two forces clashed in the forest, the Indians took cover and fired from behind trees; the British soldiers stood in ranks and attempted to fire in volleys at targets they could barely see. The Indians' war cries and the relentless slaughter of their comrades unnerved regulars and militia alike, and the battle became a rout. Braddock had several horses killed under him and took a bullet through the lungs. George Washington, his aide, escaped unwounded. An Indian later said that only three Shawnees and four Mingos fought at Braddock's defeat, all the rest being northern Indians from the Lakes.[6] The bulk of the Indian force did come from the north, but, by the time the Indian informant spoke, in 1763, the French had been defeated and it was no doubt politic to minimize the Ohio Indians' participation in the slaughter when talking to the now-victorious British.

The clashes at the Forks marked the beginning of what Winston Churchill aptly called the first world war. Known in America as the French and Indian War, the Seven Years' War (1756–63) was fought in Europe, the Caribbean, West Africa,

India, and on the high seas, as well as in North America. The conflict reverberated through Indian country and added to the tumults already battering the Indians' world. The Shawnees and many other Indian people inhabiting the Ohio Valley had already lost homelands and were not about to let it happen again without a fight. But they were careful in choosing their fight, fought for their own reasons, and were ready to change sides if and when circumstances changed.

Northern Indians, around the Great Lakes, had developed alliances with the French since the late seventeenth century: Indians needed French trade goods and guns; the French needed Indian furs. When the contest for dominance in North America came to a head, France needed Indian warriors and Great Lakes Indians logically sided with the French. The Shawnees had many ties to the Great Lakes tribes and often fought alongside them in battle against the British, but they were not so deeply connected or committed to the French. British trade goods from the east made their way into Shawnee villages as often as French trade goods from the north. The Shawnees and their neighbors were more interested in preserving their independence and controlling the terms of their dealings with all outsiders than with maintaining alliance with any single power. They backed the power most likely to help them secure their lands and independence. After Braddock's defeat, the French looked like their best bet, although the Shawnees waged their own war. South Carolina's imprisonment of six Shawnee warriors captured on a raid against the Catawbas in 1753 also helped provoke the Shawnees' declaration of war against the English. Their raiding parties began to range the frontiers of Pennsylvania and Virginia, burning cabins, lifting scalps, and taking captives.[7]

The Shawnees and their allies captured hundreds of men, women, and children during the war. Shawnees regularly took captives, both Indian and white, binding them with ties of sacred buffalo hair. Captives might be ritually tortured or ransomed but more often the Shawnees "dispers'd them amongst themselves and treated them very kindly."[8] They adopted them into their communities. Sometimes, a captive's fate hung in the balance while the captors made up their minds; other times, raiding parties carrying buffalo hair cords went out specifically to bring captives home for adoption. Jonathan Alder's experience during the Revolutionary War was typical of many captives during the French and Indian war. Taken prisoner when he was nine years old, Alder was adopted by a Mingo warrior and his Shawnee wife. His adoptive mother stripped him naked, washed him from head to foot, all the while talking to him in Shawnee, and then dressed him in a calico shirt, breechclout, leggings, and moccasins. Alder lived with them until they died. A young Virginian named McMullen, captured in 1790, was led into Chillicothe singing, with his face painted black. He was then washed and dressed in clean clothes, and a belt of wampum was placed over his head when he was adopted.[9] Like the United States citizenship ceremony, the ritual was intended to transform a person's identity. In Shawnee eyes, the captives were now Shawnees. Adopted children often grew up thinking of themselves as Shawnees, and even those who returned home retained fond memories of their adopted parents. It was not unusual to find "white Shawnees." In the winter of 1757, for instance, a Shawnee chief sent a messenger to Sir William Johnson. The messenger was "Peter Spelman a German named in the Shawanese Language Ooligasha, who has lived these seven years past amongst the Indians."[10]

French and Indian forces racked up a string of early victories, but the British struck back. William Pitt took over as prime minister and pursued the war with new vigor and new strategies. He increased British subsidies to German allies to keep French armies bogged down in Europe, and he devoted greater efforts and resources to defeating the French in North America. In July 1758, the British captured Louisbourg overlooking the mouth of the St. Lawrence River. In August, they captured Fort Frontenac on Lake Ontario, disrupting French supply lines to the West. British agents made peace overtures to Ohio Indians, assuring them their lands would be safe. Ohio Indians listened. Realizing they could not defend the Forks of the Ohio without the support of the local Indians, the French blew up Fort Duquesne in November.

The British war effort proved unstoppable in 1759. In July, the British captured Fort Niagara, severing supply routes between Montreal and other posts on the Great Lakes and dealing another blow to French standing in Indian country. In September, British redcoats captured Quebec after a dramatic victory that cost the lives of both the British general, James Wolfe, and the French general, the Marquis de Montcalm. In November, the Royal Navy destroyed the French Atlantic fleet and won command of the seas. That decided it: Britain could pick off France's overseas possessions, French forces in Canada could expect no reinforcements, and France's Indian alliance in the West would wither from lack of supplies. In 1760, British armies converged on Montreal and the French in Canada surrendered.

As the French war effort collapsed, Indians pursued new diplomatic initiatives. In April 1760, Shawnees met with the British in council at Fort Pitt, which the British built on the ruins of Fort Duquesne. The Shawnee speaker, Missiweakiwa, reviewed how they had come to that point: "God who made all things gave us this Country and brought us through this Ground," he said; God gave the English "a country beyond the water." When the English first arrived on the coast the Shawnees "gave them land to sit down upon and plant corn." The settlers kept coming and the Shawnees kept making room for them until they were pushed "up here on the high land." Then they began to think the English "wanted to deprive us entirely out of our country." When the English and French clashed on Indian land, "You both said it was for the good of the Indians that you fought; but we think you both fought for our country." Nevertheless, Missiweakiwa said they would put aside all evil thoughts and "burry the bloody Hatchet."[11] In August, the British at Fort Pitt promised to trade with the Shawnees and their neighbors and assured them they would not deprive them of their lands if they behaved as "faithful allies."

Fort Pitt was far more formidable than Fort Duquesne had been. The pentagon-shaped stronghold was an impressive symbol of British power and a clear sign of British intentions. The redcoats were here to stay. The British army built or reoccupied a dozen more forts in Indian country between 1758 and 1762. Indians resented the presence of the garrisons and what they represented, and they knew better than to believe the British when they assured them they had no designs on their lands. In fact, the main threat to Indian lands came not from the redcoats but from colonists the redcoats could not control. Now that the "French and Indian menace" had been removed, settlers crowded west into the Ohio country. The Ohio Company resumed its activities. Even when the army tried to eject squatters, their efforts were inadequate to the task. Many of the intruders had developed a hatred of Indians during the war.

Indians expected the British to lubricate their diplomacy

with gifts, as the French had done. Instead, Britain, on the brink of financial ruin at the end of the most expensive war it had ever fought, cut back on expensive gifts. The British commander-in-chief, Jeffery Amherst, saw no reason to negotiate with Indians, refused to curry their favor with gifts, and made clear his contempt for them. Indian country braced for conflict. The Seneca chief Guyasuta advocated united Indian resistance and Seneca war belts began to circulate among the tribes. Colonel Henry Bouquet warned Amherst in the spring of 1762 that the Shawnees—"that inconsiderable & proud Tribe"—would not give up their prisoners and seemed more inclined to war than peace. Other reports said they were resolved "to carry on a War against the English while one of them remain'd."[12] An outbreak of disease in Shawnee country in the fall—reports spoke of 100 dead at the Lower Towns in September, 180 in October[13]—may have tempered Shawnee hostility, for a time.

In December, Indian agent George Croghan's deputy, Alexander McKee, returned to Fort Pitt from Shawnee country with news that some of the chiefs were on their way with some prisoners and the Shawnees would deliver all their captives in the spring. The Shawnees, Delawares, and Senecas said they never intended to make war on the English, "but Say it's full time for them to prepare to Defend themselves & their Country from us, who they are Convinced Design to make War on them." If the English did not have hostile intentions, they reasoned, why would they refuse to sell them powder and lead? "How it may End, the Lord Knows," wrote Croghan.[14]

Early in 1763, Croghan sent McKee to the Lower Shawnee Town to announce that peace had been made. Although McKee did not know that the final treaty between Britain and France had been signed in Paris on February 10 (the news did not reach America until the spring), he told the Shawnees that Britain and France had stopped fighting and the French had given up Canada and the Ohio country. McKee was a good choice for the errand: As the son of a Shawnee mother he might just escape being tomahawked for bringing such news. The Shawnees were shocked and furious to hear that France had handed over their lands to Britain without even consulting them: They were undefeated and the French had no right to give up their country to anyone. They would not give up their prisoners until they learned more about this outrage. A delegation promptly set off for Fort Pitt.[15] Their fears were confirmed. At the Peace of Paris France ceded to Britain all its claims in North America east of the Mississippi. It ceded its lands west of the Mississippi to Spain, mainly to prevent them from falling into British hands. French commanders in Indian country announced that the war was over and that French and English hearts were now one, but the peace terms alarmed rather than reassured the Indians.

Among the Delawares, a prophet named Neolin gave

spiritual force to Indian discontent, preaching that they could redeem themselves as Indians only by casting off alien influences and returning to traditional ways. Shawnees who refused to listen to Christian missionaries listened to Neolin's teachings that sacred power could be restored.[16] An Ottawa war chief named Pontiac turned anti-British sentiment into direct action: At Detroit in April 1763, he urged delegates from the Three Fires Confederacy—the Ottawas, Potawatomis, and Ojibwas—to expel the British. In May, Pontiac's warriors tried to take Detroit by surprise. The British foiled the attempt, forcing a siege that lasted six months. Indian warriors took every British post west of the Appalachians except Detroit, Niagara, and Fort Pitt; they carried the war from the Great Lakes and the Mississippi to the Appalachians, and they killed five hundred British soldiers and hundreds of settlers. A dozen years before American colonists did it, American Indians revolted against the British Empire.

Shawnees and Delawares laid siege to Fort Pitt. "You marched your armies into our country, and built forts here, though we told you, again and again, that we wished you to move," the Delaware chief Turtle's Heart told the fort's commander. "My Brothers, this land is ours, and not yours."[17] General Amherst responded by ordering his officers to take no prisoners and advocated using germ warfare. Indians who came to negotiate at Fort Pitt in the spring of 1763 were given blankets from the smallpox hospital, and smallpox ravaged

Indian villages that summer.[18] Meanwhile, Sir William Johnson worked to prevent the war from spreading, to split the Indian confederacy, and to pit the Iroquois against the western tribes.

In August, Colonel Henry Bouquet marched a small army of fewer than five hundred men to the relief of Fort Pitt. Shawnee, Delaware, and Mingo warriors ambushed them at Bushy Run in western Pennsylvania and fought a vicious two-day battle. By evening on the first day, the exhausted British soldiers were pinned down on the crest of a hill behind hastily constructed barricades of flour sacks. Only a desperate feint the next morning saved the command from being overrun. Bouquet ordered the middle of his line to fall back, giving the impression of collapse, and then, as the Indians surged forward to grasp the victory, his troops flanked them with deadly volleys of musket fire. The Shawnees and their allies withdrew and Bouquet's battered force limped on to Fort Pitt.

While British redcoats battled the Indians in America, the British government in London pushed through plans to prevent such war from happening again. The Royal Proclamation of October 1763 defined the Appalachian Mountains as a boundary line between Indian lands and colonial settlements. Only the Crown's representatives acting in open council with Indian nations could negotiate transfers of Indian land, and only licensed traders were permitted to operate in Indian country.

Disease, shortage of supplies, and the different agendas of the various tribes undermined the Indian war effort. Shawnees sent word in June 1764 that they were ready for peace, although they still blamed the British for the war. The Indians had warned the redcoats not to take possession of Detroit, they said, but the first thing the British did was build a fort there: "That was one Chief Reason for entering into a War against you, as we had sufficient reason to think you intended taking our country from Us."[19] William Johnson made peace with the Senecas, who had played a key role in the war, but many Ohio Indians kept fighting. John Bradstreet marched south from Fort Niagara in the summer of 1764 and offered the tribes preliminary, and unauthorized, peace terms. Bradstreet's superiors thought the Shawnees and Delawares had fooled him and negotiated only to ward off his assault: "They have been treating with us on one side, and cutting our Throats on the other," said General Thomas Gage, who replaced Amherst as commander-in-chief of British forces in North America.[20]

In the fall Bouquet marched west from Fort Pitt with fifteen hundred men and dictated peace terms to the Delawares, Shawnees, and Mingos. The French could no longer assist them, he said; the other tribes had made peace, and the Iroquois had joined the British. "We now surround you, having gained possession of all the waters of the Ohio, the Mississippi, the Miamis, and the lakes. . . . It is therefore in our power totally to extirpate you from being a people." As the price of peace, Bouquet demanded that within twelve days the Indians hand over their prisoners, even those who were adopted or married into the tribe.[21] In November, the Indians delivered two hundred captives and the Shawnees promised to bring in one hundred more in the spring. They displayed "the utmost reluctance" in parting from their captives. Many of the prisoners wept as they were separated from their adopted families.[22]

In May 1765, a delegation of fifteen Shawnee chiefs, together with forty-five warriors and their women and children, joined Seneca and Delaware delegates in conference with the officers of the British garrison at Fort Pitt.[23] The Shawnees crossed the Ohio River with the English captives they were returning. They entered the fort "beating a Drum, and singing their Peace Song agreeable to the Antient Custom of their Nation, which they continued till they entered the Council House." They promised to carry out all the agreements they had made with the British in preliminary peace talks. The next day, Lawoughqua, their speaker, opened a new era in Shawnee foreign policy when he addressed the English as "fathers." The use of kinship terms of address was common, and crucial, in Indian diplomacy, indicating the relative standing of the parties involved. The Indians had customarily addressed the French as "fathers," and now the Shawnee speaker bestowed that term on the British. The British were pleased

"The Indians delivering up the English Captives to Colonel Bouquet."
Abiding by the terms of their treaty, grieving Shawnees and Delawares
return captive children to the British in 1764. The "liberation" proved
a heartbreaking experience for the captives as well as for the Indian
families who had adopted them. Engraving from William Smith, An
Historical Account of the Expedition against the Ohio Indians in
the year 1764 *(Philadelphia, 1766). Dartmouth College Library.*

to be acknowledged in this way, reading into it a recognition of their authority, as the United States would do when it promoted use of the term "Great Father" to indicate the president. But in many Indian societies "father" was a figure who bestowed care and protection on his children rather than one who commanded obedience. Lawoughqua explained, although it is not certain that the British officers caught the distinction. The Shawnees were pleased to be called children of the king of England, he said. It showed the English intentions toward them were upright, "as we know a Father will be tender & kind to his Children." In case the redcoats missed the point, Lawoughqua added "we hope our Father will take better care of his Children than has heretofore been done." As evidence of their good faith, the Shawnees agreed to provide hostages and to send emissaries to the Illinois country to win over the western tribes to the peace.

Then they turned to the matter of the English captives whom they now returned as they had promised Colonel Bouquet. "Father, Here is your Flesh and Blood," said Lawoughqua. "They have been all tyed to us by adoption, and 'tho we now deliver them up to you, we shall always look upon them as our relations whenever the Great Spirit is pleased that we may visit them." He handed the British a large string of wampum and continued: "We have taken as much care of these prisoners as if they were our own Flesh and Blood. They are become unacquainted with your Customs and manners, and therefore fathers we request you will use them very tender and kindly which will be a means of inducing them to live contentedly with you." He handed the British a six-row wampum belt, commending the captives to their care.

Then Lawoughqua presented a seven-row wampum belt symbolizing the new era in Shawnee-British relations: "Here is a Belt with the figure of our Father the King of Great Britain at one End, and the chief of our Nation at the other, this represents them holding the Chain of Friendship and we hope that neither side will let slip their hands from it so long as the Sun and Moon gives light." Two months later the Shawnees ratified their agreement and made a final treaty with William Johnson.[24]

As promised, a Shawnee escort accompanied George Croghan on his peace mission to the nations of the Wabash and the Illinois. Croghan's mission almost ended in disaster when a war party of Kickapoos and Mascoutens attacked them, and killed and wounded several people, including three of the Shawnees. But once the Kickapoos realized they had killed Shawnees and might bring down vengeance on their heads, they hastened to make amends and allowed Croghan's party to proceed.[25] Lieutenant Alexander Fraser, who had gone ahead of Croghan to prepare the way for peace with Pontiac and the Illinois tribes, also had a close call when a Shawnee chief named Charlot Kaské threatened his life.

According to some accounts, Charlot Kaské was of

Shawnee-German parentage and had a white wife. But he was a staunch opponent of the British. He visited the French governor in New Orleans and told the Indians that it was only a matter of time before the French would recover and join them in expelling the redcoats. He led the Indian resistance movement in the West long after Pontiac had given up. This appears to have been the chief "called by the French Charlow, and by the English Corn Cobb," who confronted a detachment of the Forty-second Regiment (the Black Watch) as it headed down the Ohio to take possession of Fort Chartres and the Illinois country in the fall of 1765.[26] "In a stern voice he demanded who we were, what business we were going on, and what brought us into his Country, as he call'd it." He denied hearing that the British had made peace with the Shawnees and "ordered us to go back immediately." The chief said the French governor at New Orleans had told him the English wanted "to dispossess you of your lands, cheat you and, at last, extirpate your whole Race." History seemed to support the Frenchman's warning. "You English, when you first came amongst us, only settl'd upon the Sea Coasts and ask'd for a very small quantity of land," Charlot said. "But as more and more of you came over and as you increased, you ask'd again for a span length and then for a step, which we poor Indians always gave you. Now you envy us every good spot of Land we have, even for our hunting."

It was a familiar refrain in Indian diplomatic encounters

with Europeans, but as a Shawnee Charlot drew on a long tribal history of movement and dispossession on the cutting edge of the English frontier. He told the officers that his father had told him always to be an enemy to the English, "for if you do not you will soon see them much more numerous than ever Indians were upon this River, and they will increase so fast as to drive you at last all out of the Country." When his father told him this, he said, "I was only so high, (keeping his hand but a small height from the ground). As I grew higher and higher (raising his hand still), my hatred increased as I grew up."

The Indian scouts accompanying the soldiers intervened to assure the Shawnee chief that the English hearts were now good and he should not believe French lies. Reluctantly, Charlot agreed to let them pass, telling them that "since he saw we were headstrong and mad enough to attempt what we would never succeed in, he would give good words to the people we met with and it would fare the better for us." The detachment continued on its way and took possession of Fort Chartres. With the British victory secured, it seemed that the Shawnees had found peace and found a new father.

They were to be disappointed on both counts.

3

THE TRAVAILS OF CORNSTALK

NIMWHA, BROTHER OF the Shawnee chief Cornstalk
and a prominent leader in his own right, had made peace
with the British at Fort Pitt in the spring of 1765. But he had
few illusions about his new friends. Now, three years later,
he was back at Fort Pitt, in conference with the British. "You
think yourselves Masters of this Country," he told them,
"because you have taken it from the French, who, as you
know, had no Right to it, as it is the Property of us Indians."[1]
Nimwha understood the threat that British power posed to
Shawnee land and sovereignty. Like Cornstalk, he endeavored to protect that land and sovereignty by peace and diplomacy, but the tumult engulfing the Ohio Valley rendered
such efforts futile.

The Royal Proclamation of 1763 promised protection of Indian lands west of the Appalachians, but the line in the mountains did not hold. Settlers and speculators regarded lands in the West as the fruits of a hard-won victory over the French and Indians, and they resented and ignored the attempts of a distant government to restrict their access to the prize. Virginia land speculators like George Washington, Thomas Jefferson, and Patrick Henry saw Britain's interference with their freedom to make a profit from Indian lands as an act of tyranny to be evaded if possible, resisted if necessary. Washington told his friend and business associate William Crawford that he regarded the proclamation as no more than "a temporary expedient to quiet the Minds of the Indians & [one that] must fall of course in a few years." Crawford should not miss the opportunity of hunting out good lands now, as others would do so if he did not.[2] Speculators bombarded the government with petitions for land grants in the territory that was supposed to be reserved for Indians. In late October and early November 1768, Sir William Johnson met with delegates from the Six Nations of the Iroquois at Fort Stanwix, at what is now Rome, New York. The Iroquois agreed to give up a huge area of land south of the Mohawk and Ohio Rivers and extending west as far as the Tennessee River. Johnson received a telling off from his superiors in London for exceeding his instructions and his authority, but the treaty effectively shifted the proclamation line westward, making the Ohio River the new dividing line between Indian and white land.[3]

In effect, the Iroquois diverted pressure from their own homelands by ceding most of present-day Kentucky and West Virginia as well as parts of western Pennsylvania—territory the Shawnees hunted and claimed as their own. The Shawnees were not present as participants at the treaty. A few who happened to be there protested but were silenced by the Iroquois, who claimed dominion over the ceded lands on the basis of their victories there in the seventeenth century. It suited William Johnson and the British to buy into the Iroquois position, to deal with tribes like the Shawnees through the Iroquois, and to obtain title to Shawnee lands from the Iroquois. As far as land speculators and frontiersmen were concerned, it was open season on Shawnee hunting grounds, even if the Shawnees had not agreed to their opening. The Cherokees also agreed to a new southern boundary line, first at the Treaty of Hard Labor in 1768, and then renegotiated and pushed farther west at the Treaty of Lochaber in 1770. The Shawnees again protested against the Cherokees' selling lands in Kentucky that they regarded as their hunting grounds. The two boundary lines met on the Ohio River. In the words of the late historian Wilbur Jacobs, the lines "silhouetted a huge geographical arrowhead directed to the heartland of America."[4] It was an arrowhead that produced much bloodshed. Whites went in confident that their invasion was legal; Shawnees who had never relinquished the land treated them as trespassers.

The Shawnees denounced the Fort Stanwix treaty as a deal concocted between the British and the Iroquois to steal their lands. Alexander McKee had his finger on the pulse of Indian country and kept the British informed. McKee's mother was Shawnee, he had a Shawnee wife by this time (she gave birth to their first child in 1769 or 1770), and he enjoyed the confidence of his Shawnee relatives. George Croghan said the Shawnees would tell McKee anything "as they Consider him as one of thire own people."[5] Shuttling between Fort Pitt and the Shawnee towns, McKee reported mounting anger and a growing conspiracy, with the Shawnees at its center. The Shawnees and their neighbors "complained much of the Conduct of the Six Nations giving up so much of the Country to the English without asking their Consent or Approbation." They called the Six Nations "slaves of the white people." Young warriors said it was better to die like men than be kicked about like dogs.[6]

In protecting their own lands and selling their neighbors' lands, the Iroquois forfeited their leadership role among the western tribes; in failing to protect the Shawnees' lands, the British forfeited their role as fathers. The Shawnee chief Red Hawk said the Six Nations had no more "right to sell the Country than we have." The Shawnees had listened to them while their advice was good, he said, but "their power extends no further with us." The Shawnees stepped up to build a coalition of Indian nations independent of Iroquois influence and British authority and opposed to the land sales at Fort Stanwix. Shawnee emissaries carrying messages and wampum belts traveled from the Great Lakes in the north to Creek country in the south. The Shawnees built "a very large Council House" on the banks of the Scioto River and held multitribal congresses there.[7] Despite McKee's intelligence gathering, the British were caught off guard. "The Congress held at Sciota by the Shawnese & western Nations has had more Effect than our Indian Officers thought possible to be brought about," General Gage wrote to John Stuart, superintendent of Indian affairs in the South in the fall of 1770. Spies reported that the tribes around the Great Lakes and the Wabash Valley had agreed to make peace with the Cherokees and other southern nations. The Shawnees were "the principle fomenters of the league," said Gage, and their "deputys have not worked in vain." The general was impressed: "The scheme of the Shawnese to form a confederacy of all the Western and Southern nations is a notable piece of policy, for nothing less would enable them to withstand the Six Nations and their allies against whom they have been much exasperated on account of the boundary treaty held at Fort Stanwix."[8] Stuart informed his deputies in Cherokee country that the Shawnees "are at the head of the Western confederacy which is formed upon the principle of maintaining their property in the lands obtained from the Six Nations at Fort Stanwix and prevent their being settled by white people."[9] Referring to the congress at the Scioto in a report to London, William Johnson said "the Chiefs of the most powerful Nations on the Continent were assembled for purposes that were too Interesting to be overlooked."[10]

British colonial authorities were unable to check the invasion of Shawnee lands. Among the first trespassers was Daniel Boone. He went first in 1769 in company with frontier trader John Findley and half a dozen men. They entered from North Carolina through the Cumberland Gap and spent the summer hunting in the game-filled forests of northern Kentucky. The Shawnees caught them in the fall. They killed one man but let the others go with a warning after they confiscated their furs and guns. "Go home and stay there," they told Boone and his companions. "Don't come here any more, for this is the Indians' hunting ground, and all the animals, skins and furs are ours; and if you are so foolish as to venture here again, you may be sure the wasps and yellow-jackets will sting you severely." As historian John Mack Faragher notes, by European standards it was a pretty mild punishment for poaching.[11]

The intruders returned to North Carolina in haste, but they took with them tales of the rich hunting grounds and fertile valleys beyond the mountains. Boone sneaked back into Kentucky the next spring, and made it home without the Shawnees detecting him. In 1773, he sold his farm in North Carolina and led five families and forty single men through Cumberland Gap. The Indians hit them before they were out of the mountains. A party of Cherokees and Shawnees drove off their livestock and killed six people, including Boone's eldest son, James. The intruders retreated but regrouped and returned two years later. Others followed—from Virginia, North Carolina, and Maryland. The word was out: Kentucky was a hunter's paradise. In 1773, Shawnees told Alexander McKee their hunting was poor: "the Woods covered with White People."[12]

White hunters did not behave like Indian hunters. In Europe, hunting was the sport of gentlemen; hunting for subsistence was regarded as poaching. In North America, the gentry classes worried that it might indicate a reversion to an earlier, more "savage" state of development. Almost all backcountry settlers hunted, supplementing their crops and livestock, and they learned techniques from the Indians. In their dress, appearance, ways of living, ways of fighting, and the embryonic communities they erected, they displayed so many similarities to Indians that they worried eastern colonial authorities and sometimes shocked eastern travelers. For backcountry settlers as for Shawnee Indians, prowess as a hunter became an essential marker of manhood. But backcountry settlers rarely adopted or observed the morality of Indian hunting values.

They paid scant regard to rituals and behavior the Indians said were vital if the game were to continue—game was so bountiful it was inconceivable that its supply might be finite. For Euro-American hunters killing game provided food and hides and demonstrated their mastery over the animal kingdom. They felt no kinship with animals as persons of other-than-human form and saw no need to display respect, offer prayers, or give thanks to the animals they killed, let alone ask their forgiveness. Impatient with their own government's efforts to restrict their encroachments on Indian hunting territories, they were hardly likely to let Indian practices restrict their hunting once they got there. With Indians hunting more and more to meet commercial demands, and backcountry settlers hunting without restraint, animal populations plummeted. Buffalo once roamed Kentucky in herds, but now, recalled one pioneer, "Many a man killed a buffalo just for the sake of saying so." Buffalo in Kentucky were wiped out before the end of the eighteenth century. In their place came pigs, domesticated cattle, and fences demarcating land that the newcomers called property. When the white intruders were not hunting, they were felling and burning trees, building cabins, plowing fields, planting crops, herding livestock. The very landscape changed, and many of its meanings. When Shawnees encountered the trespassers, they sometimes confiscated their kill or pelts and warned them to keep off Shawnee land and keep their hands off Shawnee game. Increasingly, more often than not, they killed them. There was more than a contest for deer meat at stake.[13]

Confronted with invaders of their hunting territories, the Shawnees handed other tribes the war axe "to hold always ready between our Leggs, they being Sure the White People intended to take all our Country from us, and that very soon." When that happened, the tribes must be ready to rise up "and defend it to the last Drop of blood." The Seneca chief Guyasuta said that 170 Shawnees had harvested their corn, packed up everything, and moved away from the Scioto rather than "be Hemmed in on all Sides by the White People, and then be at their Mercy." They "saw no other way to escape their Ruin, than by Removing from Scioto, and considering the Whites as their Enemies." Shawnee chiefs complained to Alexander McKee that white people were encroaching on their lands. The chiefs were doing their best to keep their young men in line; could not the British restrain theirs?[14]

After a series of nasty frontier skirmishes, tensions exploded in Lord Dunmore's War in 1774.[15] That spring frontier thugs murdered thirteen women and children, the family of a Mingo chief, Tachnedorus, also known as John Logan. The victims included Logan's Shawnee wife and his pregnant sister, whom the killers strung up by the wrists and sliced open, impaling the unborn child on a stake. Logan's grief became immortalized in various versions of a speech attributed to him, especially the one recorded by Thomas Jefferson in his book *Notes on the State of Virginia*. Logan took his revenge by raiding settlers in Virginia and then declared that his vengeance was satisfied. But the governor of Virginia, John Murray, Earl of Dunmore, and his associates seized on the Indian raids to drum up a war against the Shawnees. In Shawnee villages the voices of militant warriors drowned out moderate words from older civil chiefs: "Our People at the lower Towns have no Chiefs amongst them but all are Warriors," Shawnees reported in 1774.[16] Richard Butler, a trader who had lived among the Shawnees, did not believe they intended to fight at this point, despite provocations that would have driven a Christian people, let alone "a Savage People," to war. He could not, however, speak to their future intentions.[17]

The British feared the conflict might spread into a general Indian war and moved quickly to dismantle the coalition the Shawnees were building. William Johnson worked on the Iroquois and John Stuart worked on the Cherokees to make sure they kept out of the conflict. Shawnee delegates trying to rally allied tribes had their belts rejected, and Shawnee emissaries who traveled to Onondaga, the central council fire of the Iroquois, were told they could expect no assistance. In one instance the Iroquois threw the Shawnees' belt back at them.[18] The British Indian department's divide-and-rule tactics effectively isolated the Shawnees. According to David Zeisberger, the Wyandots asked the Shawnees why they were going to war when all the other Indian nations were at peace. The Shawnees denied it but rumors that they were preparing to move farther west seemed to confirm it. A Shawnee chief indicated as much, but first, he said, "they would turn around and defeat those who were closest to them, because this was the Shawnee way."[19] Virginia went to war against them and the Shawnees went to war virtually alone.

Many Virginians had been waiting for a chance like this. In a circular letter calling for volunteers, Colonel William Preston urged men to turn out and defend their lives and properties. "We may Perhaps never have so fair an Opportunity of reducing our old Inveterate Enemies to reason," he said. "It will be the only Method of Settling a lasting Pace with all the Indian Tribes Arround us, who on former Occasions have been Urged by the Shawnese to ingage in a War with Virginia. This useless People may now at last be Obliged to abandon their Country, Theire Towns may be plundered & Burned, Their Cornfields Distroyed; & they Distressed in such a manner as will prevent them from giving us any future Trouble." There were other incentives as well; there would be valuable plunder, and "it is said the Shawnese have a great Stock of Horses."[20] For their part, the Shawnees distinguished between Pennsylvanians and Virginians, saying they intended to rob the former but kill the latter.[21]

In August, Major Angus McDonald, a veteran of both

the 1745 Jacobite Rebellion in Scotland and the French and Indian War in America, led an expedition against the Shawnee towns on the upper Muskingum River. The Virginians burned cabins and cornfields, killed several people, and took three scalps and one prisoner.[22] But this was only a prelude to the main campaign. While Governor Dunmore led one army of fifteen hundred men down the Ohio from Fort Pitt, General Andrew Lewis led another force of about eleven hundred down the Kanawha River. They intended to rendezvous, cross the Ohio, and launch a combined assault on the Shawnee villages on the Scioto. Chief Cornstalk reputedly urged his warriors to seek peace, and on the evening before the battle offered to go and talk with the Virginians. But the Shawnees would not listen to him. So Cornstalk and his war chiefs Black Hoof, Black Fish, Blue Jacket, and Puckeshinwa rallied the warriors from the Scioto villages. Together with some Mingo and other allies, they were able to muster no more than seven hundred men. Hopelessly outnumbered, they pinned their hopes on being able to defeat one of the advancing armies before they joined forces.

Crossing the Ohio by rafts at night, the Shawnees attacked Lewis's army at sunrise on October 10 at a place called Point Pleasant. By sunset the forest floor was as red as the leaves on the trees. Shawnees and Virginians agreed that it was a hard-fought and desperate battle. At first the Shawnees pushed the Virginians back. Then Virginian reinforcements arrived and the Shawnees in turn had to retreat, until they formed a line behind logs and trees from the bank of the Ohio to the bank of the Kanawha River. Colonel William Christian said that, urged on by their chiefs, the Shawnees fought with bravery that "exceeded every man's expectations." Colonel Charles Stuart, who fought in the battle, credited Cornstalk with "great military skill." He recalled: "I could hear him the whole day speaking very loud to his men; and one of my company, who had once been a prisoner, told me what he was saying; encouraging the Indians, telling them 'be strong, be strong!' " But the Shawnees began to run out of powder and shot and sheer weight of numbers made it a lost cause. Toward sundown Cornstalk began to withdraw his exhausted warriors across the Ohio. The Virginians suffered 75 killed, including Charles Lewis, the general's brother, and 140 wounded. When they walked over the battlefield the next morning, they counted 20 Indian dead on the ground and scalped the bodies. They later found a dozen more concealed in one place. The Indians, said Stuart, "confessed that they had thrown a number into the river in time of the battle; so it is possible that the slain on both sides, were about equal." John Norton, who spoke with Shawnees early in the nineteenth century, said that they suffered about 30 men killed and "lost the Pouch which contained the War Charm."[23]

Several "white Shawnees" fought against the Virginians at Point Pleasant. George Collett, John Ward, and Tavernor

Ross were in the Shawnee ranks. Collett was heard exhorting the Indians to fight on against "the white Damnd. Sons of bitches." After the battle, his body was found among the Indian dead. His brother, who was in the Virginian army, identified his body. John Ward's natural father, also in the Virginian army, was killed in the battle. Ward himself survived. In 1792, he fought in a skirmish with a party of Kentucky militia that included his brother; a year later he was mortally wounded in a clash where another brother fought on the opposing side. Tavernor Ross, on the other hand, eventually left his Shawnee relatives and returned to live in the American settlements.[24]

Colonel Stuart may have inflated the Shawnee losses, but forcing the Shawnees from the field constituted victory enough. Lewis's army consisted mainly of young volunteers, but despite having sustained more than 20 percent casualties, they crossed the river eagerly, "bent on destroying the enemy." Had they not been restrained by the governor's orders, Stuart believed, "they would have exterminated the Shawanese nation."[25]

Cornstalk returned to the Shawnee towns and called a council to consult on what to do next. He "upbraided" the Shawnees for not letting him make peace the evening before the battle. Now the Big Knives were advancing on their homes. "He said, then let us kill all our women and children, and go and fight till we die." When no one responded, Cornstalk got up, struck his tomahawk in the post at the center of the council house, and announced he would go and make peace. Rather than deal with Lewis and his vengeful army, he chose to meet with Governor Dunmore at Camp Charlotte.[26] Matthew Elliott, an Irishman who had fought against the Shawnees at Bushy Run but who had been trading with them for the past nine years and had earned their confidence, agreed to carry the message to Dunmore.[27]

Peace proved expensive. Dunmore demanded that the Shawnees give up their lands south of the Ohio and send four hostages to Williamsburg as a guarantee of future good conduct. One of the hostages was Cornstalk's son, Wissecapoway. A young Englishman who saw them on their way to Williamsburg described the hostages as "tall, manly, well-shaped men, of a copper colour with black hair, quick piercing eyes, and good features." Their heads were shaved except for a long scalp lock and their faces painted with vermilion. They had silver rings in their noses, and the tops of their ears were slit and extended with brass wire so that they hung down and touched their shoulders. They wore white men's clothing, "except breeches which they refuse to wear," preferring their traditional loincloths.[28]

Cornstalk endeavored to keep the peace he made, and some Shawnees became reconciled to the loss of their lands south of the Ohio. Others never did. A chief named Kishkalwa, who fought at Point Pleasant, was said to be unwilling to fight against the Americans again or to become embroiled in the growing conflict between Britain and the colonies. He led many of the Thawekila band south where they joined other Shawnees living among the Creeks. They later returned to the banks of the Ohio and from there moved again, this time crossing the Mississippi into Spanish territory.[29]

Kishkalwa. Kishkalwa led his people south after the defeat at Point Pleasant, returned to Ohio to fight in Blue Jacket's confederation, then migrated west to Missouri. This portrait was painted by Charles Bird King when Kishkalwa visited Washington in the 1820s. Engraving from Thomas L. McKenney and James Hall, The Indian Tribes of North America *(1836–44). Dartmouth College Library.*

When the American Revolution broke out, Indians in the Ohio country understood that it was a war over Indian land as well as a war for independence. They heeded British warnings that the Americans intended to take their country and destroy them. Their best chance lay in siding with the British, who had offered at least token protection for Indian lands, rather than with the Americans, who were clearly hell-bent on taking them. Shawnee chiefs told the Virginians in July 1775, "We are often inclined to believe there is no resting place for us and that your Intentions were [sic] to deprive us entirely of our whole Country."[30] At first, like most Indian nations, they hoped to stay out of a conflict they regarded as a British civil war. Located between the frontiers of Virginia and Kentucky on the one hand and the British and their Indian allies closer to Detroit on the other, the Shawnees were in a hard place. Reports that summer said they were constantly debating the war but divided about what course to follow. At a treaty with the Continental Congress at Fort Pitt in the fall, Shawnee chiefs joined Wyandots, Delawares, and Senecas in agreeing to remain neutral.[31]

Yet in April 1776, a Shawnee chief accompanied a delegation of fourteen northern Indians who traveled to Cherokee country to incite them to war. British Indian agent Henry Stuart was in the Cherokee town of Chota when they arrived. Painted black, they made a dramatic entry. They had traveled seventy days to get there, through country that used to be Shawnee and Delaware hunting grounds but was now "thickly inhabited and the people all in arms." The delegates argued their cause in the council house. The Shawnee deputy was the last to speak. He produced a nine-foot purple wampum belt, painted red as a sign of war. He recited the grievances of the Shawnees and other nations, particularly their cruel treatment at the hands of the Virginians. The Shawnees had once possessed lands stretching almost to the Atlantic Ocean and the Indians once held the whole country; now they barely had enough ground to stand on. "Better to die like men than to dwindle away by inches," he declared. The older Cherokee chiefs, who had seen war and tasted defeat, sat silent, but the warriors led by a young chief named Dragging Canoe accepted the Shawnee war belt. It proved to be a disastrous step. Cherokee war parties attacked the settlers who encroached on their lands, but armies from Virginia, Georgia, and the Carolinas immediately retaliated, burned Cherokee villages and crops, and then dictated peace terms. Rather than surrender, Dragging Canoe led his warriors deep into present-day Tennessee and continued the fight from the Chickamauga River and Lookout Mountain. Militant Shawnees and Chickamauga Cherokees made common cause.[32]

In July 1776, a war party of two Cherokees and three Shawnees captured Jemima, the daughter of Daniel Boone. It was a Sunday afternoon, and tired of being confined in

Boonesborough, she and two other teenage girls took a canoe out on the river. The Indians seized them and set off for the Shawnee villages in the Ohio country. When the alarm was raised, Boone and other pioneers immediately gave chase. Picking up the trail and pushing hard, they caught up with the Indians on the third day, attacked them in camp, and rescued the girls. The Indians fled, two of them wounded, possibly mortally. Despite the trauma of their ordeal, Jemima insisted the Indians were "really kind to us." The event became a staple of frontier lore and provided James Fenimore Cooper with material for *The Last of the Mohicans*.[33] That summer, Matthew Elliott went to the Shawnee towns on the Scioto River with a request that the Shawnees meet the Americans in a treaty at Fort Pitt in the fall. He came back predicting a general Indian war.[34]

But in meetings with George Morgan, the American Indian agent at Fort Pitt, Cornstalk and other Shawnee chiefs asserted that their people intended to remain neutral and preserve their friendship with the white people. Admittedly, some young men had already raised their hatchets, but Cornstalk said they were fools who had been misled by the Mingos and other troublemakers. He told Weepenachukthe (the White Deer, the Shawnees' name for Morgan), "All our old wise Chiefs are dead, & we look on ourselves but as Boys in Wisdom," but when they spoke with him the dark clouds dispelled and they could see things clearly. More than six hundred Indians showed up at the Treaty of Fort Pitt that fall and confirmed the Ohio River as the boundary of their lands. Cornstalk took the opportunity to send a message to Congress. He asked Morgan to take down his words and forward his speech to Philadelphia. Congress had asked several times that the chiefs tell them the cause of their complaints against the Americans. "We always thought your Wise men could see into the causes thereof," said Cornstalk, but since they asked, he would "open my hand and pour into your hearts the cause of our discontent in hopes that you will take pity of us your younger Brethren, and send us a favorable Answer, that we may be convinced of the sincerity of your Professions." While Morgan's quill scribbled across the page, Cornstalk explained that American land thefts struck at the core of Shawnee life.

> When God created this World he gave this Island to the red people and placed your younger Brethren the Shawnese here in the Center. Now we and they see your people seated on our Lands which all Nations esteem as their and our heart. All our lands are covered by the white people, and we are jealous that you still intend to make larger strides. We never sold you our Lands which you now possess on the Ohio between the Great Kenhawa and the Cherokee River, and which you are settling without ever asking our leave, or obtaining our consent. Fool-

ish people have desired you to do so, and you have taken their advice. We live by Hunting and cannot subsist in any other way. That was our hunting Country and you have taken it from us. This is what sits heavy upon our Hearts and on the Hearts of all Nations, and it is impossible for us to think as we ought to whilst we are thus oppressed.[35]

Cornstalk, Kishanosity, Moluntha, the war chief Oweeconne, and other Mekoche chiefs continued to assure Morgan of their desire for peace and blame the Mingos for misleading their young warriors. But Cornstalk had little authority beyond his own Mekoche division by this time and he warned that he could not restrain his warriors: "When I speak to them they will attend for a Moment & sit still whilst they are within my Sight. —at night they steal their Blankets & run off to where the evil Spirit leads them," he said.[36] In March 1777, Moravian missionary David Zeisberger, who regularly passed on information to the Americans, wrote in his diary: "The warriors are no longer listening to the Chiefs who want peace; they want to have war."[37] Several towns moved away from the Scioto to the Miami River and its tributaries to avoid the coming conflict.

The chiefs at Fort Pitt said they intended to separate from those who wanted war and to build a new town. In March, the Delaware Council reminded the Shawnees of what had befallen them three years previously and invited them to settle at the Delaware capital, Coshocton. Cornstalk planned to move his people closer to the Delawares for safety.[38] But the war party was gaining in strength in Shawnee villages. That same year, Shawnee warriors accepted a war belt from Governor Henry Hamilton at Detroit and joined raids on the American frontier.[39]

In early October, Cornstalk visited the American garrison at Fort Randolph on the Kanawha River, at the site where he had fought the Virginians exactly three years earlier. A Shawnee chief called Red Hawk and another Shawnee called Petalla accompanied him. Colonel Charles Stuart, who was at the fort, recalled what happened. Cornstalk apparently made no secret of the Indians' disposition. He said he was opposed to joining the war, but the current was so strong against the Americans that the Shawnees would have to run with the stream, in spite of all his efforts. Hearing this, the post commander, Captain Matthew Arbuckle, decided to take the three Shawnees hostage, to try to prevent the nation from joining the British. A month later, Cornstalk's son Elinipsico came to see what had happened. Father and son "embraced each other in the most affectionate manner." Meanwhile, however, soldiers brought in the body of a young man who had been killed and scalped. Some of the militia immediately yelled, "Let us kill the Indians in the fort." Despite Stuart and Arbuckle's efforts to stop them, they burst into the building where the Shawnee hostages were held. As Cornstalk rose to meet them they shot him dead in a hail of bullets. His son was shot as he sat on a stool, and Red Hawk was gunned down as he tried to escape up the chimney. "The other Indian was shamefully mangled," said Stuart, "and I grieved to see him so long in the agonies of death." In what was probably an imaginative creation, Stuart attributed to Cornstalk a premonition of his death just an hour before it happened. "When I was a young man and went to war, I thought it might be the last time, and I would return no more. Now I am here amongst you; you may kill me if you please; I can die but once; and it is all to me, now or another time." The governors of Virginia and Pennsylvania sent urgent messages to the Shawnees; George Morgan conveyed Congress's regret; and Patrick Henry denounced the murders, but it was too little and too late. General Edward Hand recognized, "If we had anything to expect from that Nation it is now Vanished."[40]

But Cornstalk's Mekoches remained predominantly neutral and kept "hold to the Chain of Friendship" their chief had forged with the Americans. Cornstalk's sister, Nonhelema, actually left her people and moved to Fort Randolph. She frequently acted as an interpreter and messenger for the Americans, and on occasion supplied the garrison with cattle. Known to the Americans as Catherine or "the Grenadier Squaw," she incurred the enmity of her people and lived in poverty around Pittsburgh. In her old age she petitioned

Congress for support and for two thousand acres on the Scioto where she once lived and where her mother was buried. The committee appointed to consider her petition concluded she had "a just claim on the humanity of the people of the United States." They recommended she be allowed "one suit or dress of Cloaths including a blanket per annum, and one ration of provisions each day during her life."[41] Nimwha, Kishanosity, Oweeconne, and seventeen Mekoche families moved to Coshocton. The Delaware town was becoming a refuge for Indians who were trying to remain neutral. Unfortunately, this was a war that tolerated no neutrals.[42]

4

NEGLECTED LIKE BASTARDS

CORNSTALK'S MURDER SWELLED the ranks of the Shawnee militants. Shawnee runners carried war belts, and news of Cornstalk's death, through Indian country. Following paths they knew well, they drew allies as far afield as Ojibwas and Creeks into the Indians' most extensive intertribal coalition yet.[1] More Shawnees accepted the war belt offered by British governor Henry Hamilton at Detroit. In the fighting that followed, they weathered American assaults on their villages and defeated American forces, only to be defeated themselves by peacemakers in Paris.

In January 1778, Shawnees captured Daniel Boone, again. Black Fish, who had been a rival of Cornstalk for the position of principal chief, led a large war party into Kentucky and headed for the settlement at Boonesborough. En route they surprised Boone and a party of men at the salt springs on the Licking River. Caught off guard in a snowstorm, Boone persuaded his twenty-six companions to surrender rather than throw their lives away and indicated that he would be willing to talk Boonesborough into surrendering in return for guarantees of good treatment. The Shawnees headed north with their captives. They made Boone run the gauntlet, between two lines of people striking him with clubs and sticks, but after they reached Chillicothe most of the captives were adopted into Shawnee families. Black Fish adopted Boone to take the place of a dead son. Boone recalled that Black Fish and his wife were kind to him and that he grew attached to his adoptive family. But he also dissembled to buy time for Boonesborough. When the chance came he made good his escape, returned to Boonesborough, and helped organize its defenses. Most of the other captives also eventually managed to escape. Shawnee warriors raided Fort Randolph and the Kanawha Valley in the spring, and lay siege to Boonesborough in September but the settlement held out. Some of Boone's fellow settlers regarded his actions with suspicion, believing he had surrendered his men to save his own skin and seemed much too friendly with the enemy, but a militia court-martial vindicated his conduct. Despite Boone's dissembling, Black Fish maintained warm relations with his adopted son.[2]

In March 1778, Alexander McKee, Matthew Elliott, and

Simon Girty, one of three brothers who had been captured and had grown up with the Indians and then played intermediary roles on the frontier, went over to the British. Leaving Pittsburgh in the dead of night, they crossed the Ohio country to Detroit. There, they formed the core of the British Indian department in sustaining the Shawnee war effort during and after the Revolution.

Meanwhile, some Shawnees continued to migrate rather than continue fighting the Americans. Kishkalwa, who had led his band south into Creek country and then back to Ohio, now moved west of the Mississippi. Beginning around 1779 or 1780, Yellow Hawk and Black Stump led some twelve hundred Shawnees to Missouri, where they took up lands near Cape Girardeau under the auspices of the Spanish government.[3] To modern American eyes, Shawnee migrations beyond the Mississippi may seem like little more than shifting domicile, as thousands of Americans do every year; after all, the area the Shawnees moved to became United States territory a little more than twenty years later. But at the time the Shawnees migrated, Louisiana Territory was held by Spain. Their movement is more analogous to, say, refugees from Mexico moving across the Rio Grande today, or migrants from the United States moving to Canada; it represented a political decision as well as a geographical relocation.

The Shawnees who remained in Ohio were mainly

Chillicothes and Mekoches, together with members from other divisions who refused to leave their homelands. The Mekoches may have hoped to remain neutral, but the war would not leave them alone. Daniel Brodhead, the commander at Fort Pitt, sent the Shawnees a speech in 1779 advising them to listen to peace and ignore the intrigues of British agents, but the warriors burned it in defiance.[4] British officers warned the Shawnees not to listen to the Americans who would certainly take possession of their country "if You hang your Heads and remain quiet spectators."[5] Shawnees rarely did that. Their emissaries carried the war hatchet south to Creek country.

Thomas Jefferson, governor of Virginia during the war, wanted to see the Ohio Shawnees exterminated or driven from their lands, and he advocated turning other tribes against them.[6] Almost every year now American troops from Kentucky invaded Shawnee country and burned crops and villages. In 1779, John Bowman led a campaign against Chillicothe. A handful of warriors repelled and harassed the attackers, but Black Fish was wounded and died a week later. A severe winter followed but Shawnees hit the frontiers again in the spring. They raided settlements in the Ohio Valley, forced the Americans to abandon Fort Randolph, and effectively closed the Ohio River to American traffic. Shawnee warriors routinely ambushed settlers traveling downriver on flatboats, sometimes assisted by white Shawnees who lured the emigrants closer to shore. The British reported that the Shawnees and their allies brought scalps to Detroit every day.[7] Shawnee warriors also joined a multitribal assault into Kentucky led by British officer Henry Bird, along with McKee, Elliott, and the Girty brothers. They captured two settlements, Ruddell's and Martin's Stations, and took more than three hundred prisoners. Among the captives were a twelve-year-old boy named Stephen Ruddell, and his six-year-old brother Abraham. Their parents and siblings were soon released, but the two boys remained with the Shawnees for years. They gave Stephen a Shawnee name, Sinnamatha or Big Fish, and he became a close friend of Tecumseh, who was about his age.

In retaliation, George Rogers Clark invaded Shawnee country with one thousand men. The Shawnees burned Chillicothe rather than see it fall to the Big Knives; they made a stand at Piqua on the Mad River and did not withdraw until Clark turned his six-pound cannon on the village council house where many of the people had taken refuge. The Americans killed some old people they found hiding in the cornfields and spent three days burning the crops. Some men plundered Shawnee graves for burial goods and scalps. Shawnee losses were slight but the destruction of their corn hit them hard that winter.[8] Shawnees now looked to the British for assistance. Refugees filtered into Detroit asking for food and shelter. "We see ourselves weak and our arms feeble to the force of the enemy," said one Shawnee chief in a council held there in spring 1781. " 'Tis now upwards of Twenty Years since we have been alone engaged against the Virginians."[9]

The British general Lord Cornwallis surrendered to the French and Americans at Yorktown in October 1781, effectively bringing an end to the war on the eastern seaboard. In the West, however, the war continued unabated. The following March, American militia perpetrated an infamous massacre at Gnadenhütten, a Delaware Indian mission community on the Tuscarawas River. The congregation of converts to the Moravian faith—and therefore pacifists—offered no resistance. Ninety-six men, women, and children knelt singing psalms and praying as the frontier heroes systematically clubbed them to death. Once again, American atrocities helped bolster Indian resistance. Later that spring, Shawnee warriors assisted the Delawares in routing an American invasion force under Colonel William Crawford, George Washington's associate in speculating in Indian lands. The Delawares captured Crawford, tortured him, and burned him to death in retaliation for Gnadenhütten. David Zeisberger said the Shawnees tortured and burned any prisoners they believed had participated in the massacre.[10]

Shawnee war parties ranged the frontier in the summer of 1782. In August, Black Hoof and Blue Jacket, together with Simon Girty and warriors from several tribes, attacked Bryan's Station at present-day Lexington, Kentucky, and then ambushed a Kentuckian force at Blue Licks on the Licking

River. Daniel Boone, who was with the Kentuckians, urged caution as the militia advanced but Hugh McGary, an Indian-hating loudmouth who had lost relatives at Indian hands, spurred them on with taunts of cowardice. The Kentuckians ran headlong into the trap the Indians had set and seventy of them died, including Boone's son, Israel.[11]

George Rogers Clark invaded Shawnee country again in the fall. According to Daniel Boone, who accompanied the expedition, he burned five villages, "entirely destroyed their corn and other fruits, and spread desolation through their country." Most of the warriors were absent when Clark attacked. "Every man who was able to crawl" went out to fight, along with boys, old men, and women. The Kentuckians, whom the Indians called "the white Savages Virginians," were reported to have committed atrocities. But the Shawnees refused to be drawn into open battle and evidently suffered few casualties.[12]

With each American invasion, Shawnees pulled back, congregating in new towns on the Auglaize and Maumee Rivers in northeastern Ohio, beyond Clark's reach. Some families took up residence with the Delawares; others moved south to Cherokee and Creek country; still others migrated west of the Mississippi. Physical movement was a relatively simple operation for the Shawnees—they could rebuild their lodges in a few days—but leaving familiar sites took an economic and emotional toll.

As some Shawnees left, other Indians—Mingos, Senecas, and Cherokees—joined Shawnee communities to continue the war effort. The British dispensed guns and support. Matthew Elliott, Alexander McKee, and James Girty—all of whom had Shawnee wives and extensive kinship ties in Shawnee villages—acted as intermediaries and served as conduits through which supplies flowed to Shawnee villages. They accompanied Shawnee warriors into battle and spoke in Shawnee councils. Americans offered rewards for McKee and the Girty brothers and blamed them for inciting the Shawnees, but American actions, not British intrigues, drove Shawnees to war. Americans regarded the Shawnee towns as lairs of renegades and terrorists; for Indians, they were strongholds of freedom.

Then, just as it seemed the Shawnees were winning their war, Britain snatched them from the jaws of victory. Suddenly, British officers and agents were urging the chiefs to restrain their warriors and look forward to a new era of peace with the Americans! In council at Detroit that summer, Major De Peyster roundly criticized the Shawnees for spilling American blood. A Shawnee chief, Snake, explained that the victims were horse thieves the Shawnees had tracked down, but De Peyster would have none of it. "The times are very Critical," he explained; "the World wants to be at Peace & its time they should be so." If the Shawnees chose to fight now, "it must be an affair of your own, as your Father can take no part in it." The king had made peace and was honor-bound to keep it, "and can afford you no assistance if you foolishly bring mischief upon yourselves."[13] The Americans put it more bluntly, telling the Shawnees: "Your Fathers the English have made Peace with us for themselves, but forgot you their Children, who Fought with them, and neglected you like Bastards."[14]

The Peace of Paris in 1783 ended the American War of Independence. It did not include or even mention the Indian nations that had fought in the war, but it dramatically affected them. Britain handed over to the United States all territory east of the Mississippi, south of the Great Lakes and north of Florida. The peace did not bring peace to Indian peoples nor did it bring an end to their struggle for independence. With an empty treasury at the end of a long war, the United States government needed to convert Indian country into American real estate, either by war or by treaty. It concentrated its efforts north of the Ohio, where individual states relinquished their western land claims to the national government. The Shawnees had fought to defend their hunting territories south of the Ohio, but now they were told their land north of the river had been handed over to their enemies. Shawnee country lay right in the path of American expansion.

European colonial powers had dealt with Indian peoples by following the protocols of council-fire diplomacy and lubricated negotiations with a steady supply of gifts. Like the

French before them, the British learned that compromise, conciliation, and respectful dealings were often more effective than force, or the threat of force, in a world where Indian power was real and where Indian nations usually had a choice of European allies. Although the Crown was unable to enforce its policy on distant frontiers, Britain tried to regulate and restrict encroachment on Indian lands. Americans fought for independence, in part at least, to remove those restrictions. With Britain defeated, the United States was anxious to impress on the Indians that a new era had dawned, and that Americans were a new breed of men, who were not to be trifled with. Like Britain, the United States preferred to achieve its goals by treaty rather than by war, and obtain Indian lands by purchase rather than by risky and expensive military campaigns. But it insisted the United States had acquired all territory east of the Mississippi by right of conquest and demanded that the tribes acquiesce. Meanwhile, Shawnee emissaries traveled through Indian country trying to keep alive the alliance that had resisted American expansion during the Revolution and urging the tribes to remain united in defending the Ohio country. "It is the Gift of the Great God who made all things," said a Shawnee speaker at a council at Sandusky in September 1783, "and we have already spilt the best of our Blood defending it."[15]

Shawnees were among a delegation of some two hundred Indians who visited St. Louis the next summer. They told the

Spanish governor they were already feeling the impact of the American victory. The Americans, they said, were "a great deal more ambitious and numerous than the English." They descended on the Ohio Valley "like a plague of locusts," drove out the Indians, and built great settlements where their villages had once stood. American victory meant continued warfare and hunger for the Indians; it was, they said, "the greatest blow that could have been dealt us."[16]

Commissioners from "The Thirteen Fires" (the United States) traveled into Indian country. They employed the rhetoric and symbols of council-fire diplomacy, but they went to browbeat, not to negotiate. At the Treaty of Fort Stanwix in the fall of 1784, delegates from the Six Nations met commissioners from the United States, as well as from New York and Pennsylvania. With troops at their back, the Americans announced that they were masters of all Indian lands and could do with them as they thought fit. They demanded huge cessions of Iroquois country as the price of peace. "You are a subdued people," they told them. Still divided by the war and now abandoned by their British allies, the Iroquois delegates agreed to cede much of Seneca land in western New York and Pennsylvania as well as all their territory west of Pennsylvania, and they gave six hostages to guarantee their compliance.[17] When they returned home they were met with scorn. The Six Nations in council refused to ratify the treaty on the grounds that the delegates were not authorized to cede the territory, but the United States proceeded as if the treaty were valid. The Oneidas and Tuscaroras had supported the Americans during the war, but their lands, too, were soon up for grabs.

In January 1785, at the Treaty of Fort McIntosh, United States commissioners demanded large cessions of land from the Wyandots, Ojibwas, Delawares, and Ottawas. When the Indians objected that the king of England had no right to transfer their lands to the United States, the Americans reminded them they were a defeated people. The delegates made their marks on the treaty dictated to them. Of the Indian tribes north of the Ohio River who had fought against the Americans during the Revolution, only the Shawnees refused to make peace.

Shawnees knew from past experience that peace for them could only be bought with land. As it was, Americans were pouring into Shawnee country, "settling our Country & building Cabbins in every place." In May 1785, with Simon Girty interpreting, Kekewepellethe, also known as Captain Johnny, told the Americans, "You are drawing so close to us that we can almost hear the noise of your axes felling our Trees and settling our Country. According to the lines settled by our forefathers, the Ohio is the boundary, but you are encroaching on the grounds given to us by the Great Spirit." The Shawnees had no objection to dealing with American traders, "But it is clear to us that your design is to take our country from

us." If the American government did not stop its people crossing the Ohio, the Shawnees would "take up a Rod and whip
them back to your side." Kekewepellethe declared, rather op-
timistically, "We people of colour are united so that we make
but one man, that has but one heart and mind."[18] In September, Shawnee, Delaware, and Mingo chiefs told Alexander
McKee: "We mean to defend ourselves to the last man, before
we give up our lands."[19] Unfortunately, not even the Shawnees
could maintain such a united front.

The United States realized that no peace in the West
would last if it did not include the Shawnees, and it dispatched
emissaries to find Shawnees who would make peace. About
150 Shawnee men and 80 women finally came to meet the
American commissioners at Fort Finney in January 1786.[20] In
1765, Shawnees had arrived at Fort Pitt beating drums and
singing the song of peace to reach an accommodation with
the British. In 1786, Shawnees arrived at Fort Finney in the
same way. The oldest chief, Moluntha, a Mekoche civil chief,
led the procession, beating a small drum and singing, followed
by two young warriors each carrying the stem of a pipe,
painted and decorated with eagle feathers and wampum, and
by other dancing warriors, all "painted and dressed in the
most elegant manner," reported commissioner Richard Butler.
The Shawnee men entered the council house by the west door,
the women by the east door, and the dancing warriors waved
the eagle feathers over the commissioners. Kekewepellethe

gave a short speech and the chiefs shook hands with the commissioners, but the warriors and women held back. "The reason they give," wrote Butler, "is that the heads of the people should be on an easy and familiar footing, but that the warriors and women, who are the strength of the nation, more distant till peace is certain." Nonhelema, "the Grenadier Squaw," was there—Major Ebenezer Denny compiled a vocabulary of Shawnee words based on interviews with her during the conference.

Most of the Shawnees who came to Fort Finney were Mekoches. After the Revolution they had returned their war belts to the British, signifying their intention to remain at peace. They were the most conciliatory division of the Shawnees, and their traditional responsibilities included healing and negotiation. The Americans they met, however, were in no mood for conciliation. Richard Butler had been a trader among the Shawnees, spoke their language, and had two children by a Shawnee woman, but he had fought with Colonel Henry Bouquet against the Shawnees in 1764 and was a veteran of the Revolution. George Rogers Clark, the other American commissioner, had made a name for himself as an Indian fighter during the Revolution and led assaults on Shawnee villages in 1780 and 1782. At the siege of Vincennes in 1779, he had tomahawked Indian prisoners within sight of the British garrison and tossed their still-kicking bodies into the river: "To excel them in barbarity," he declared "is the only way to make war upon Indians."[21] Clark had little patience for Indian diplomacy, preferring to dictate terms with the threat of force. "I am a man and a Warriour and not a councillor," he had told Indians on the Wabash River in 1778; "I carry in my Right hand war and Peace in my left."[22] The negotiations at Fort Finney graphically illustrated the contrast between the European and American ways of conducting diplomacy in Indian country.

The proceedings opened with traditional speeches of welcome, smoking peace pipes, and dining. But this was not a meeting between equals. The Americans were determined to negotiate from a position of strength. Richard Butler said "that many of the young fellows which have grown up through the course of the war, and *trained like young hounds to blood*, have a great attachment to the British; . . . the chiefs of any repute are and have been averse to the war, but their influence is not of sufficient weight to prevent them from committing mischief, which they regret very much."[23] In return for peace, the commissioners demanded hostages to ensure Shawnee compliance and offered to grant the Shawnees portions of their own lands. Kekewepellethe replied that it was not the Shawnee custom to give hostages: "When we say a thing we stand to it, we are Shawanese." As for the land, he continued, it was not for sale: "God gave us this country, we do not understand measuring out the lands, it is all ours. You say you have goods for our women and children; you may keep your goods, and give them to the other nations, we will have none of them." The Americans "were putting them to live on ponds, and leaving them no land to live or raise corn on." The Shawnees would agree to the Ohio River as their boundary and nothing else. He handed the commissioners a black wampum belt. When they refused to accept it, he laid it on the table.

The commissioners refused to budge. They reminded the Shawnees that the Americans had defeated the British and the country now belonged to the United States. They had burned Shawnee villages before and they would do it again if necessary. The Shawnees must choose between "the destruction of your women and children, or their future happiness." Taking his cane, Clark knocked Kekewepellethe's wampum belt onto the floor and ground it under his boot. The Americans then withdrew "and threw down a black and white string" of wampum, symbolizing the choice between war and peace.

Moluntha urged his people to reconsider. When the council reconvened, the Shawnees gave the commissioners a white belt and begged them to have pity on the women and children. They then grudgingly accepted the American terms and ceded their tribal lands east of the Great Miami, which meant they gave up most of southern and eastern Ohio, including their towns on the Mad River. Moluntha, Oweeconne, and Painted Pole (sometimes called Red Pole) all signed the treaty. The American commissioners were pleased with themselves. "From the local situation of the Shawnees and the ascendancy they have over the other Indian nations," they wrote as they transmitted the treaty to Congress, "their friendship is of more importance to the weal of the Citizens of the United States than that of any other tribe of Indians in the Western Territory."[24] But the Shawnee chiefs at the treaty warned them: "This is not the way to make a good or lasting Peace to take our Chiefs Prisoners and come with Soldiers at your Backs."

There would be no peace for the Shawnees. Many who did not attend the conference were outraged by the terms, scorned those who had accepted them, and repudiated the treaty. Some refused to give up their captives as required by the treaty. Younger warriors accused Moluntha and the older chiefs of selling out to the Americans. Moluntha sent the Americans messages explaining that he was doing all he could to carry out the promises he made and bring the Shawnees around to peace, but it would take time. The people were scattered and, he explained, "It is not with us as it is with you, for if you say to a man do so why it must be done, but consider we are a lawless people and do nothing with our people only but by fair words." He asked the Americans to be patient.[25]

They were not. Before the year was over, Benjamin Logan's Kentucky militia conducted "a wild scampering foray" into Shawnee country. They burned several Mekoche villages.

Most of the warriors were away, responding to rumors of another invasion by Clark. "Logan found none but old men, women and children in the towns," said Ebenezer Denny; "they made no resistance; the men were literally murdered."[26] At Moluntha's village, the old chief met them carrying a copy of the Fort Finney treaty, while his people hoisted an American flag. Nonhelema, who consistently worked for peace despite the murder of her brother, Cornstalk, was there. The Kentuckians were rounding up their prisoners when Hugh McGary pushed his way forward to Moluntha and asked him if he had been at Blue Licks. Not understanding, the old man apparently nodded and smiled. McGary buried his hatchet in his skull and the Kentuckians destroyed the town.

Any hope of real peace between the Shawnees and the Americans died with Moluntha. That November, delegates from a dozen Indian nations assembled in council at Brownstown, near Detroit. With the Mohawk Joseph Brant eloquently arguing the need for a united front, the tribes adopted a common policy in dealing with the aggressive new nation that seemed intent on dividing the tribes, gobbling up their land, and destroying their lives. From now on, they informed Congress in a message sent in December, they would deal with the United States as members of a united Indian confederacy, not as individual tribes. As they had in the 1760s and the Revolution, the Shawnees stepped forward to play a leading role in a multitribal coalition.

5

BLUE JACKET AND THE
NORTHWESTERN CONFEDERATION

EVEN AS THE Indian delegates at Brownstown were making their bold resolution, Congress was laying out plans and procedures for dividing up their lands. Following ideas put forward by Thomas Jefferson, Congress in July 1787 issued the Northwest Ordinance, a blueprint for national expansion. As the thirteen American colonies had grown, they had come to resent their colonial status and had taken up arms to cast it off. How could the new American nation prevent history from repeating itself as western territories grew in the same way? The Northwest Ordinance provided the solution. Unlike Britain's colonies, United States territories would not suffer permanent inferior status. In time, they would take their place in the Union on an equal footing with the other states. The Old Northwest, the region that today encompasses half a dozen states, would be surveyed, divided into territories and lots, sold, and settled. Each territory would have its own territorial government, with a governor, an elected assembly, and a court. Once its population reached sixty thousand, the territory could petition to become a state. Eventually, more than thirty states entered the Union this way.

The ordinance pledged the nation to observe the "utmost good faith" in its dealings with the Indians. Their lands would not be taken from them without their consent and they would not be attacked except "in just and lawful wars authorized by Congress." Yet the ordinance committed the nation to expansion onto Indians lands: New states would be formed northwest of the Ohio River, which the Indians wanted as a barrier to white settlement. The Shawnees would not negotiate away the land God had given them. Clearly, there would be "just and lawful wars authorized by Congress."

In retrospect, American victory in those wars seems inevitable, and American advance across the Old Northwest irresistible, perhaps even preordained. Some Americans back then talked in those terms, too, but there were times when the outcome must have seemed in doubt as the Shawnees and their allies turned back one American army and destroyed another. According to John Norton, who admittedly may have been influenced by talking to Shawnees, in this war, "The Shawanons were sometimes the leaders, and always the most active agitators in every enterprise."[1] No one played a greater role in the Indian resistance than the Shawnee war chief Blue Jacket.[2]

Born in the early 1740s, Blue Jacket, or Waweyapiersenwaw, has not received the attention he deserves. His historical reputation has tended to be overshadowed by that of the Miami war chief Little Turtle, with whom he led the northwestern confederacy, and by Tecumseh, who built another confederacy. A nineteenth-century story (perpetuated by some twentieth-century writers) that Blue Jacket was actually an adopted white captive named Marmaduke van Sweringen obscured his accomplishments as an Indian leader. In reality, Blue Jacket's role in leading the Indian confederacy seems to have equaled if not surpassed that of Little Turtle, who became renowned after the war was over, and his influence on the younger Tecumseh may have been substantial.

Blue Jacket fought during the Revolution. Most likely a member of the Pekowi division, he split with Cornstalk and the Mekoches in 1777 and established his own town near the headwaters of the Mad River as a bastion of Shawnee resistance. With a French father-in-law and living close to Detroit, Blue Jacket had connections with French traders and British officers and was evidently not a cultural hardliner in his personal life and tastes: He owned livestock, trafficked in alcohol, owned black slaves, and sent his son to Detroit for an education. Blue Jacket and his French-Shawnee wife slept in a four-poster bed and ate with silver cutlery. Thomas Ridout, taken captive by Shawnees in 1788, saw Blue Jacket's home: "a fine plantation, well stocked with cattle."[3]

But Blue Jacket had a formidable reputation as a war chief. Captive Oliver Spencer called him "the celebrated Blue Jacket" and said he was considered "one of the most brave and most accomplished of the Indian chiefs." He described him as a muscular six-footer with an open and intelligent countenance; "the most noble in appearance of any Indian I ever saw." On the day Spencer saw him Blue Jacket wore a British officer's scarlet frock coat with gold epaulets, a colored sash around his waist, and red leggings and moccasins. He wore a large silver gorget and a medallion of King George III suspended from his neck. Spencer heard that he held a British officer's commission. He had a fine-looking wife and handsome daughters, "and his two sons, about eighteen and twenty years old, educated by the British, were very intelligent."[4]

The Blue Jacket family inhabited a perilous world. Southern Ohio was not a safe place for Shawnees. American forces attacked Chillicothe four times between 1779 and 1790. (The Shawnees rebuilt it several times with the same name in different locations.) Some two hundred Shawnees and Delawares left their villages on the Miami in the summer of 1787 and moved beyond the Mississippi; others followed. Tecumseh's elder brother Chisekau led the family to Missouri for a time, before returning across the Mississippi and taking up residence among the Chickamauga Cherokees in their mountain strongholds in Tennessee. (He joined them in fighting the Big Knives and was killed in 1792.) Most Shawnees moved northwest to the Maumee River, closer to British supplies from Detroit and closer to the towns of their Miami allies. Blue Jacket and Kekewepellethe both established towns on the Auglaize River.[5]

Yet even as they pulled out of range of American assaults, the Shawnees continued to draw the line at the Ohio River. When Arthur St. Clair, the first governor of the Northwest Territory, called a meeting of the tribes at Fort Harmar (present-day Marietta) on the Muskingum River in January 1789, Delawares, Wyandots, Ojibwas, Ottawas, Potawatomis, and Sauks attended, but the Shawnees refused. Joseph Brant stayed away as well. The treaty St. Clair offered basically confirmed the earlier cessions at Fort McIntosh, although with a new provision designed to undermine the fragile Indian confederacy: If the Shawnees continued to cause trouble and refuse peace, the Wyandots would dispossess them of lands they had granted them, "and take the country into their own hands." Twenty-eight Indian delegates affixed their names to the treaty.[6]

In 1790, General Josiah Harmar left Fort Washington (present-day Cincinnati) with an army of almost fifteen hundred men, mainly militia from Kentucky and Pennsylvania, and headed for the Indian towns at the headwaters of the

Maumee River. The Americans burned more crops and villages, including Chillicothe, but the Indians pulled back, leaving empty shells for the invaders to destroy. Harmar's force lacked discipline and groups frequently broke off to strike different targets and grab plunder. Blue Jacket and Little Turtle assembled six hundred warriors and struck back. They defeated parties of militia in two engagements and constantly harassed the enemy. Order and morale began to disintegrate as the Americans retreated. Only a lunar eclipse—which the Ottawas interpreted as a bad omen—prevented the Indians from following up with a major attack. As it was, the army limped back to Fort Washington leaving 183 men killed and missing. The Indians sustained fewer than a dozen casualties.[7]

Soon after the victory, Blue Jacket was in Detroit, urging the British to weigh in and support the Indians in their war. They had defeated the Americans and were determined to defend their country, but they needed help to keep their forces assembled in one place. He asked the British to send traders to the Indians' villages, provide food and clothing for families who had lost their homes, and dispatch soldiers to encourage the war effort. The commander at Detroit promised to do what he could, but he had no authority to commit troops, "as I am only a Small Finger on the hand of your Father at Quebec."[8] Blue Jacket had not forgotten that Britain had left the Indians high and dry at the end of the Revolution, and he understood that the redcoat garrisons on the frontier were there to protect imperial interests, not Indian interests. Yet those interests intersected in the dozen years following the Revolution as Britons and Indians alike worked to curb the expansion of the aggressive young republic.

At the Peace of Paris, Britain had agreed to hand over to the United States various posts scattered along the Great Lakes frontier "with all convenient speed." In fact, Britain held on to the posts for another thirteen years, citing American infringements of treaty provisions as justification. The official British stance during the renewed wars between the Indians and the United States was to remain neutral. Indian leaders made repeated requests for help and Joseph Brant traveled to England to renew high-level connections (he had visited London in 1775) and argue the Indians' case. But the government gave evasive replies. Britain wanted peace between the Indians and the United States and hoped to exert its influence in mediating a peace. But the British, like the Indians, felt there could be no peace so long as the United States insisted on taking Indian land. In fact, British ministers hoped that a neutral Indian state might be constructed in the Old Northwest that would serve as a buffer between Canada and the United States. Britain played a delicate diplomatic game: trying to avoid war with the United States while at the same time urging the tribes to remain united in defense of their lands and cultivating them as allies in case war broke out. Britain was prepared to advise and supply the Indians but would not give open assistance that would draw it into renewed war with the United States.[9]

The task of implementing British frontier policies, and of explaining them to the Indians, fell to the British Indian department. Initially formed in 1755, the Indian department expanded after British victory in the French and Indian War brought many more tribes into its orbit. Sir William Johnson, superintendent of Indian affairs in the North until his death in 1774, had established the department on a firm footing in Iroquois country, and members of Johnson's extended family continued to dominate the upper echelons of the service. In the aftermath of the Revolution, however, the course of events and the center of Indian affairs shifted westward, and the Shawnees eclipsed the Iroquois as leading players. Britain relied increasingly on agents operating at the new hub of Indian affairs. According to one British captain, who was probably exaggerating, most of the officers in the British Indian department had Shawnee wives or mistresses.[10] Alexander McKee and Matthew Elliott both had Shawnee wives, and both men exerted influence in tribal councils as well as on British Indian policy. McKee distributed supplies to the Indians but that was as far as Britain was willing to go. When a second American army invaded Indian country in the fall of 1791, Blue Jacket would fight without redcoats.

President George Washington and his secretary of war, Henry Knox, chose Arthur St. Clair, a veteran of the Revolution, to lead the army. With more than two thousand men, St. Clair was to advance toward the Maumee River, defeat the Indian confederacy, and build a string of American forts to control the territory. Blue Jacket and Little Turtle rallied their forces and seized the initiative. Simon Girty counted 1,040 warriors as they set out to do battle. "The Indians were never in greater Heart to meet their Enemy, nor more sure of Success," he wrote to Alexander McKee; "they are determined to drive them to the Ohio."[11]

Rather than pull back and nip at the army's flanks, the Indians decided to meet the enemy head-on in a pitched battle. Blue Jacket had fought at Point Pleasant in 1774 when the Shawnees had launched a dawn assault against a superior force, and he opted for the same strategy now against St. Clair. According to John Norton, the lead in the battle "was given to the Shawanons." Advancing in half-moon formation, the warriors reached the woods on the edges of St. Clair's encampment before daylight. Caught off guard and unnerved by the suddenness of the assault and the war cries of hidden enemies, the militia crumbled almost as soon as the Indians opened fire. Indian marksmen picked off officers, adding to the confusion in the ranks. St. Clair had two horses killed under him. Colonel Richard Butler, who had bullied the

Shawnees into accepting the American terms at Fort Finney, was mortally wounded and scalped; according to John Norton a Shawnee warrior tomahawked him. With men falling on all sides and discipline disintegrating, St. Clair abandoned his wounded and his equipment and led the survivors in a desperate retreat. Once they cleared the Indian lines, it became a headlong flight. More than 600 soldiers were killed, as well as 30 female camp followers; almost 300 more were wounded. The Indians lost no more than 35 men. St. Clair's army abandoned horses, wagons, artillery, tents, and muskets, and the victorious warriors plundered and mutilated the dead. Back in the Shawnee villages after the battle, captive Oliver Spencer saw a warrior strutting around wearing an infantry officer's coat with silver epaulets on his shoulders "and a watch suspended from each ear."[12] It was the single biggest defeat ever inflicted by Indians on the United States, and it effectively destroyed the new nation's only army. Compared with St. Clair's defeat, George Custer's disaster at the Battle of the Little Bighorn eighty-five years later was a skirmish and a minor setback.

The United States was in a precarious position. Britain watched from the wings, waiting for the American experiment in republican government to fail, and now hoped to push for the creation of a neutral Indian barrier state. Washington appointed General Anthony Wayne to build a new army and to finally get the job done in Indian country. The government appropriated $1 million to fund it. Despite his nickname, "Mad Anthony," which he had earned during the Revolution, Wayne set about the task with methodical determination, recruiting and training soldiers and developing a new army—he called it his legion—to be an effective fighting force in Indian country.

Meanwhile, Blue Jacket and other emissaries traveled to the Great Lakes and the Mississippi, calling nations farther west to join the confederacy that had scored such a stunning victory. Recruits gravitated to the confluence of the Auglaize and Maumee Rivers, an area known as the Glaize, where Blue Jacket, Kekewepellethe, and other confederacy leaders had built towns. Among those who returned to join the confederacy was Tecumseh, coming home to Ohio after his brother's death in the South. The Glaize became a multitribal community as well as the nerve center of the confederacy.[13] Henry Knox characterized the resistance movement as Miami and Wabash Indians, together with "a banditti, formed of Shawanese and outcast Cherokees."[14]

With its army in shambles, the United States opted to negotiate. In summer 1792, it sent peace feelers via an Iroquois delegation headed by the noted Seneca orator Red Jacket. Almost one thousand Indians from the confederated nations assembled in council at the Shawnee villages on the Auglaize River to hear the Americans' offer. Besides the Shawnees, Miamis, Delawares, and Wyandots, the core of the confederacy, there were Ottawas, Ojibwas, and Potawatomis from the Great Lakes; Sauks and Foxes from the upper Mississippi; Creeks and Cherokees from the South; Conoys, Nanticokes, and Mahicans from the East; and Iroquois deputies from the Six Nations in New York and the Seven Nations in Canada. Alexander McKee and other British Indian agents stood by as observers, although Hendrick Aupaumut, a Mahican who attended the meetings as an emissary from the United States, accused McKee of unduly influencing the outcome.

It was the end of September before all the delegates finally arrived. Red Jacket stood up to address the assembly. The Americans would be willing to compromise and might accept the Muskingum River as the boundary line, he explained. But the Shawnees saw no need to compromise. Messquakenoe or Painted Pole reminded Red Jacket in no uncertain terms that while the Iroquois had been sitting by doing nothing, the Shawnees and their allies had twice defeated American armies. The Senecas had visited Philadelphia and now were doing the Americans' dirty work and trying to divide the confederacy. Demanding that Red Jacket "speak from your heart and not from your mouth," Painted Pole picked up the strings of wampum on which Red Jacket had spoken and threw them at the feet of the Seneca delegation. Red Jacket was sent packing with his answer: The confederated nations would accept no boundary but the Ohio

River. The meetings at the Auglaize illustrated the toll that almost twenty years of war had taken on the authority of the Shawnee civil chiefs. Traditionally, civil chiefs sat in the front ranks at councils, with the warriors and women behind them. At the Auglaize, Shawnee war leaders sat in front of civil chiefs at the councils. Hendrick Aupaumut reported that it was now the Shawnee "custom that the Chief Warriors should be foremost in doing business."[15]

After the council, the Shawnees "sent pieces of tobacco painted red to call together the Warriors" in preparation for the next American army.[16] Blue Jacket headed south with a delegation of Shawnees and his message of Indian unity. The Shawnees told the Creeks and Cherokees they must join the fight against American aggression; it was "now or never."[17] Some Creeks and Cherokees, particularly the Chickamauga Cherokees in Tennessee, made common cause with the confederacy, and the Spaniards hoped to use the Indian confederation as a defense against an anticipated American invasion of the Illinois country. A party of Shawnees went to New Orleans and from there to Pensacola, where the Spanish governor gave them presents and sent them on to Creek country. The Shawnees apparently told the governor "they would be at war with America as long as any of them should live."[18] But there was not general support in the South: The Chickasaws and Choctaws actually supplied the United States with scouts to serve against the northern nations.

As Anthony Wayne rebuilt the army and prepared for another invasion, the United States continued to pursue diplomatic options, in the hope of avoiding war by wringing concessions from the Indians, or simply to divide the confederacy in preparation for war. John Graves Simcoe, lieutenant governor of Upper Canada, was no friend to Americans but he was not far off the mark in his assessment of the situation: "It appears to me that there is little probability of effecting a Peace, and I am inclined to believe that the Commissioners do not expect it; that General Wayne does not expect it; and that the Mission of the Commissioners is in general contemplated by the People of the United States as necessary to adjust the ceremonial of the destruction and pre-determined extirpation of the Indian Americans."[19] While Wayne advanced to Fort Washington, American commissioners Benjamin Lincoln, Timothy Pickering, and Beverly Randolph traveled north to meet sixteen Indian nations in council at Lower Sandusky in the spring of 1793.[20]

The British offered to facilitate the meetings and kept them under close scrutiny, ostensibly to help move the peace process forward but in reality to ensure that Indian lands and Indian unity remained intact. While the British "hosted" Lincoln, Randolph, and Pickering, first at Niagara and then at Matthew Elliott's house on the Detroit River, delegates from the various tribes assembled at the foot of the Maumee rapids, where Alexander McKee kept a storehouse, and held their own discussions before meeting with the commissioners. Joseph Brant suggested ceding land east of the Muskingum River as a compromise solution, but with two victories under their belts, few delegates saw any reason to back down now from their insistence on the Ohio River boundary. The Delaware chief Buckongahelas indicated that McKee told them to insist on the Ohio; Joseph Brant accused McKee of orchestrating the Indians' stance. With McKee and Elliott present at the councils, the British Indian department exerted its influence through its Shawnee agents to further its plans for an Indian barrier state.[21]

Messages passed back and forth between the Indians and the commissioners, but the talks got nowhere. The Indians saw no reason to compromise and the Americans were not likely to concede while General Wayne was preparing for war. The Shawnees demanded that the Ohio boundary established at Fort Stanwix in 1768 be restored and that American settlements north of the Ohio be removed. The commissioners said that was out of the question: The Indians had ceded the lands north of the Ohio by treaty and American settlers were already living there. They suggested that the government might be willing to modify its position that the Indians' lands belonged to the United States by right of conquest. The Shawnees asked why Wayne was advancing if the United States was serious about making peace. After two weeks of fruitless negotiations, the western Indians came up with a counterproposal, no doubt with McKee's input. Money, they said, was of no value to them, and they would never consider selling the lands that provided sustenance for their women and children. There could be no peace as long as white settlers were living on their lands. However, tongue in cheek, they offered a formula for peace:

> We know these settlers are poor, or they would never have ventured to live in a country which has been in continued trouble ever since they crossed the Ohio; divide, therefore, this large sum of money, which you have offered to us, among these people . . . and we are persuaded, they would most readily accept of it, in lieu of the lands you sold them.

Add to this the vast sums the government would save by not having to raise and pay armies to fight the Indians, and there would be ample money to compensate the settlers for their labor and improvements. The Americans, they said, talked a lot about preemption and having obtained the exclusive right to purchase Indian lands from the British at the Peace of Paris. But the Indians had never given the king of England any such power and they would sell their lands to whomever they wished: "If the white people, as you say, made a treaty that none of them but the King should purchase of us, and that he has given that right to the United States, it is an affair that concerns you and him and not us. We have never parted with such a power." The Indians' only demand, they reminded the commissioners, was "the peaceable possession of a small part of our once great Country. Look back and view the lands from whence we have been driven to this spot, we can retreat no further, because the country behind hardly affords food for its present inhabitants. And we have therefore resolved, to leave our bones in this small space, to which we are now confined." Delegates from all the tribes affixed their marks to the message, except Brant and the Iroquois. Lincoln, Randolph, and Pickering packed their bags and left. There was no point trying to talk with these people. "The Indians have refused to make peace," they reported to the secretary of war.[22] General Wayne's invasion would be "just and lawful." The day the commissioners left, the Indians at the rapids held a war feast, with "the Chiefs of the Shawanoes singing the War Song encouraging the Warriors of all the Nations to be active in defending their Country." They said their English father would assist them and pointed at Alexander McKee.[23]

Wayne built Fort Recovery on the site of St. Clair's defeat and settled in for the winter. Warriors from farther west began to head home to their families but the Shawnees had nowhere to go—the enemy was encamped on their doorstep. The British helped keep the Indian alliance ready for the impending renewal of hostilities in the spring. They rebuilt Fort

Miamis on the banks of the Maumee River and, in February 1794, Sir Guy Carleton, Lord Dorchester, who was governor of Canada, told an Indian delegation in Quebec that Britain and the United States were likely to be at war within the year, in which case the boundary line "must then be drawn by the Warriors."[24] McKee and Elliott talked up the likelihood of British military support among their Shawnee relatives.

Blue Jacket and his messengers called the warriors of the scattered tribes back to the fight in the spring. In June, Blue Jacket ambushed a party of dragoons from Fort Recovery, but when the Ottawas led an assault on the fort itself, the American artillery drove them off. The Ottawas had had enough and most headed for home. Many Ojibwas and Potawatomis followed suit. The Indian confederacy lost its momentum and about half its warriors. It was no longer the force that had destroyed St. Clair three years earlier.

And Wayne, advancing methodically with a trained and disciplined army of twenty-two hundred regular infantry and fifteen hundred militia cavalry from Kentucky, was no St. Clair. As his army marched along the Auglaize River, the Shawnees and their allies abandoned the villages that had served as the core of the resistance movement. People loaded canoes and ponies and hurried away with small children; old women burdened with heavy packs struggled after them.[25] In August, Wayne built Fort Defiance at the junction of the Maumee and Auglaize Rivers, formerly the heart of the confederacy. Little Turtle saw the writing on the wall and began to advocate making the best peace they could get. Blue Jacket, Tecumseh, and the others would hear none of it. Acknowledging that this was now a fight for younger men, Little Turtle relinquished leadership of the confederacy to Blue Jacket. Blue Jacket was "commander in chief," said Jonathan Alder, who was living with the Shawnees.[26]

But Blue Jacket's confederacy was unraveling. American diplomacy and divergent tribal agendas had produced divisions in its councils, and many disheartened warriors of the Three Fires had gone home. The militant warriors who formed the core of the confederacy remained, but the Indian force was further reduced on the eve of its showdown with Wayne. Taking advantage of an area strewn with uprooted trees after a tornado at a place called Fallen Timbers, Blue Jacket drew up his warriors in battle line to fight on August 19. But Wayne's army halted and the expected battle did not take place that day. Warriors who had fasted in ritual purification before battle now began to disperse in search of food. Wayne's army appeared the next morning.

It was a lost cause. The Indian army was drawn up in the half-moon formation that had proved so effective in engulfing St. Clair's army, with the Shawnees on the left wing. But the Indians were outnumbered and outgunned. The American artillery did bloody work on their ranks. The Indians put up some stiff resistance on the left, where Blue Jacket and

Tecumseh fought, but were unable to withstand the disciplined advance of the American bayonets. Looking back in old age, an Ottawa who stayed and fought there as a young man recalled: "Our moccasins trickled with blood in the sand, and the water was red in the river."[27] Driven from the battlefield, the warriors fled to Fort Miamis, where they expected they would receive sanctuary if not outright assistance from the British garrison.

But the British were not to be trusted. Canadian and Detroit militia fought in the Indian ranks at Fallen Timbers, but Alexander McKee, Matthew Elliott, and Simon Girty watched the battle from a safe distance. They knew what would happen to them if they fell into American hands. Another white man, Charles Smith, an adopted Shawnee, was shot through the knees during the battle. When the Americans got hold of him he was "quartered alive, th' shocking to relate, nevertheless true."[28] After the battle, the gates of Fort Miamis remained barred to the Indians. Nervous about events in revolutionary France, the British government had no intention of getting caught up in a shooting war with the United States for the sake of its Indian allies. Instead, the fort's commander engaged in a war of words with Wayne. Then the American army withdrew and put to the torch the huge Indian cornfields that stretched along the banks of the Auglaize and Maumee Rivers. Wayne described this as "the grand emporium of the hostile Indians of the West." Alexander McKee claimed the Americans "left Evident marks of their boasted Humanity behind them": Besides scalping and mutilating the Indians who were killed in the battle they dug up graves, exposed the rotting corpses, and drove stakes through them.[29]

For years, Shawnees had pulled back as American armies advanced into their country, watched as the troops torched their villages, then returned or rebuilt new homes in safer locations after the enemy departed. Shawnee communities had survived the destruction of their villages. Food sources beyond the reach of American strikes and British supplies at Detroit had sustained the Shawnee war effort. Now, the British had betrayed them and stood by as Wayne's army destroyed their cornfields. "The conduct of the British Fort dispirited the Confederates much more than the issue of the battle," John Norton said. They had fought with inferior numbers, in a disadvantageous position, and had not suffered great casualties. They could fight another day and reverse the outcome of the battle, but the British betrayal "they did not know how to remedy."[30]

Many Shawnee warriors wanted to keep fighting, but the old chiefs sought accommodation with the Americans. Blue Jacket joined them. "This Chieftain," said Norton, "had been a brave and distinguished Warrior, possessing strong natural parts, that were now ripened by the experience of age, which perhaps had also damped the fire and enthusiasm of Youth."[31]

Wearing his scarlet coat with gold epaulets, Blue Jacket went to meet Wayne face to face. He agreed to the preliminary articles of peace. "In a few simple words," writes his biographer, "Blue Jacket surrendered the upper Ohio to his conquerors." Wayne was jubilant: "The famous Blue Jacket has pledged himself as a man of honor and as a war chief that he will now make a permanent peace and be as faithful a friend to the United States in future as he has lately been their inveterate enemy." In fact, Blue Jacket overstepped his authority and had to work to sell his peace to warriors he had recently led into battle. A war chief who stopped fighting should have relinquished authority to the civil chiefs; instead Blue Jacket now presumed to speak for the nation in peace talks. Many Shawnees were angered by his actions. Blue Jacket informed Wayne in private conference that Alexander McKee had told him he was betraying the Shawnees and "must now be viewed as the enemy of your people." In his own mind, Blue Jacket evidently conflated his people's interests and his own interests: The Shawnees needed peace now, and if the aging war chief was to remain a key player on the frontier, he had better cultivate relations with the Americans who had defeated him rather than with the British who had deserted him.[32]

More than one thousand Indians, including 143 Shawnees, attended the Treaty of Greenville in the summer of 1795.[33] Blue Jacket arrived late, and Painted Pole arrived later

Paytakootha, also known as Flying Clouds and Captain Reed, one of the Shawnee chiefs who signed the Treaty of Greenville, after which he moved west to Missouri. Portrait by Charles Bird King. Engraving from Thomas L. McKenney and James Hall, The Indian Tribes of North America *(1836–44). Dartmouth College Library.*

still, but at least they came. Most Shawnees stayed away, among them Kekewepellethe and Tecumseh, who remained bitterly opposed to the Americans and to the treaty. Painted Pole admitted that a few Shawnees, "who have been in the woods a long time hunting," continued to do "mischief," but he declared that the Shawnees "do acknowledge the Fifteen Fires as our father," and he offered his own father as a hostage.[34] The chiefs who attended signed away the southern and eastern two-thirds of Ohio and smaller tracts of land in Indiana. Blue Jacket, Painted Pole, Black Hoof, and Paytakootha all signed for the Shawnees. A year later, Blue Jacket and Painted Pole traveled to Philadelphia to meet President Washington. The men who had accused Red Jacket of being an American stooge were now following in his footsteps. Painted Pole died on the way home at Pittsburgh and was buried in Trinity Church graveyard. Blue Jacket returned to his people to begin a new chapter in Shawnee history. He had fought against the Americans for twenty years; now it was time to try to work with them.

6

BLACK HOOF AND THE
WAPAKONETA WAY

JONATHAN ALDER WAS living with the Shawnees when
the Treaty of Greenville was signed. It was not long before
"white people began to make their appearance amongst us."
What Alder saw was the beginnings of a population tsunami
that would transform Ohio. In 1796, there were 5,000 whites
in Ohio. Ohio became a state in 1803. By 1810, its population
had jumped to more than 230,000. Ten years later it had shot
past 580,000. By 1830, Ohio was the fourth-most-populous
state in the Union, with a population of 938,000.[1] Shawnees
who remained in Ohio had to change or be engulfed, but
what form would the change take and would it stave off disaster? The struggle over what kind of life Shawnees should
live now was fought among Shawnees as well as between
Shawnees and Americans.

In addition to taking most of Ohio by the Treaty of Greenville, the United States created the conditions to exert influence through client chiefs and exercise leverage in tribal governments. The treaty established an annuity system, offering annual payments of one thousand dollars to each of the tribes, which the chiefs would distribute to their people. Leaders who had been defeated in battle could maintain their prestige by distributing goods, but they were now dependent on the federal government as the source of those goods. In return, the chiefs were expected to promote the work of "civilization" in their communities.[2] Some Shawnees accepted such cultural transformation as inevitable and the price of progress; to their opponents, it was cultural betrayal.

After Fallen Timbers some Shawnees, mainly Kispokos, migrated with Tecumseh rather than deal with the Americans and succumb to American ways of living. They moved to Deer Creek in southern Ohio, then to the upper Miami Valley, and then to eastern Indiana. Around 1800, they joined a displaced Delaware community on the White River near the site of present-day Indianapolis. Back in his village on the Detroit River, Blue Jacket accepted bribes from the United States and was given an honorary commission in the U.S. Army. He developed a taste for his new way of life, and for strong drink. He had no love for the Americans but now he could neither lead his people in resistance nor lead them along a new path. Most Shawnees, especially Mekoches and Pekowis, accompanied the Mekoche chief Catahecassa or Black Hoof to a new town at Wapakoneta on the upper Auglaize River. Wapakoneta became a test community in another round of struggles for the Shawnees as its five hundred residents experimented with a new way of life.

Catahecassa, or Black Hoof. Artist unknown. Engraving from Thomas L. McKenney and James Hall, The Indian Tribes of North America *(1836–44). Dartmouth College Library.*

According to United States Indian agent John Johnston, who knew him in his old age, Black Hoof was born in Florida and could remember bathing in salt water when he was a boy. Johnston said he was eighty-five in 1819, and that he fought his first battle against General Braddock at the Monongahela. Since the Shawnees were "the most restless and warlike" of the Indian nations, Black Hoof "was probably in more battles than any living man in his day." Though small of stature, Black Hoof was a great orator. He lived to be more than one hundred years old, dying at Wapakoneta shortly before the tribe emigrated westward.[3]

The turn of the century was a hard time to be Shawnee. The war for the Ohio River boundary was over, and the victors quickly confirmed their hold on Ohio. Formerly the dominant force in the Indian confederacy, the Shawnees were now a defeated people. They had fought for the whole Northwest, but now they were confined on tiny reservations, and still the Americans encroached on their lands. Powerful advocates for Indian unity, they themselves were now more divided than ever. Shawnee men had traditionally demonstrated their manhood in war and hunting; now they had stopped fighting and it was increasingly difficult to feed their families as game became depleted. The United States government urged them to take on farming, a task formerly reserved to Shawnee women. The Americans promised them civilization and prosperity; what they got was poverty, alcohol, and despair.

Thomas Jefferson was a leading advocate of bringing Indians to "civilization." Jefferson was a man of many contradictions, as his writings on human rights and his record on slavery famously demonstrate. In his attitudes toward Native Americans, as toward African Americans, Jefferson can appear ambivalent, hypocritical, and duplicitous. He took what appeared to be contradictory positions on Indian relations, although at least in his own mind, he successfully reconciled them. As a scholar, Jefferson admired Indian character and customs. He recorded Indian languages, excavated an Indian burial mound near his home in Monticello, instructed Meriwether Lewis and William Clark to gather all the information they could about Indians during their expedition to the Pacific, and seems to have developed affection for individual Indians such as the Kaskaskia chief Jean Baptiste du Coigne, who named his own son Jefferson. In his book *Notes on the State of Virginia*, Jefferson recited the tragic story of Logan, whose family was brutally murdered on the eve of Lord Dunmore's War. He believed that Indians were culturally inferior but that, with proper guidance and instruction, they were capable of improvement, of becoming "civilized." In many public utterances Jefferson appeared as a concerned friend of the Indians and a champion of their rights.

But Jefferson also speculated in Indian lands, relished the opportunity to expel the Cherokees from their lands during the Revolution, and advocated destroying the Shawnees during the wars for Ohio. When he became president, he was far more concerned with dispossessing Indians than with civilizing them, and he was the architect of policies that would eventually result in Indian people being forcibly removed from the eastern United States beyond the Mississippi. He said the best government was the one that governs least, and although he did not always adhere to that principle once he was in power, his government certainly did little to uphold treaties and protect Indian lands from trespass. When Indian grievances escalated to the point of war, however, the government had no choice but to exert its power, suppress the uprising, and dictate treaties in which defeated Indians signed away more land. Jefferson's strategy for acquiring Indian lands resulted in some thirty treaties with a dozen or so tribal groups and the acquisition of almost two hundred thousand square miles of territory in nine states. Taking Indian lands was for the Indians' own good, Jefferson told himself, because it would compel them to give up hunting and become farmers. In Jefferson's vision of the future, this was the Indians' only alternative to extinction. Giving Indians "civilization" in return for land allowed the United States to expand with honor. The United States needed Indian lands in order to grow; the Indians needed American civilization in order to survive. It was a fair exchange. Indians who refused to change (and sell) were doomed, which was lamentable but inevitable. As Anthony F. C. Wallace put it, "The Jeffersonian vision of the destiny of the Americas had no place for Indians as Indians."[4]

Many Indian peoples at the beginning of the century were ready to try the path of cultural conversion, if only because the alternatives were so grim. The Cherokees of Georgia and Tennessee had seen their towns burned in wars against both the British and the Americans. Now Cherokees tried to survive by emulating their white neighbors instead of fighting them. Many wore European styles of clothing, lived in log homes, plowed fields, fenced their lands, and grew corn and cotton. They had sawmills, gristmills, and blacksmith shops, and they owned looms and spinning wheels. Some held slaves. In time, they developed a written language, established a newspaper, and adopted a written constitution, modeling their government on that of the United States.

Shawnees had fought tooth and nail against American expansion, but they, too, had regularly adopted elements of the white man's technology and culture. Now, many felt, it was necessary to adopt more. As white people flooded into what had once been the Shawnee homeland and American laws and practices affected Shawnee lives, perhaps it was time for Shawnees to learn to live like their new neighbors. Shawnee men must learn to plow fields and tend cattle instead of hunting; Shawnee women must learn to spin and weave instead of farming. For many it was a hard choice. It was not the Shawnee way, but it was a way for Shawnees to survive.

Migration offered another way. About one thousand Shawnees lived in Missouri. Originally migrating west to escape British and American domination, they had settled in territory claimed by Spain. The governor of Louisiana granted them land near Cape Girardeau in 1793, and they established several villages in the area. Shawnees who had been living in Creek country joined them before the end of the century, along with others from Ohio who continued to filter across the Mississippi. Most of the original migrants were members of the Thawekila division, although increasing numbers of Pekowis and Kispokos joined them. The migrants hoped they could preserve their way of life in the West beyond the reach of American aggression and assaults on their culture. They joined with other Indian peoples who had been displaced from the eastern woodlands to the Missouri-Arkansas region, and as they had in the Ohio country in the 1780s and 1790s, they built multiethnic coalitions and communities. They fought against the Osage, Quapaw, and Caddo peoples living in the area for access to hunting grounds. The Spaniards wanted to use migrant Indians as a buffer against both the Osages and the Americans, and encouraged more Shawnees to move west.[5] Then Spain transferred the Louisiana Territory to Napoleon Bonaparte, and, in 1803, Napoleon sold it to the United States. The Missouri Shawnees were under American jurisdiction again, and the United States had a vast new country to which eastern Indians could be removed.

Unlike the western Shawnees, Black Hoof believed that his people could and must survive in Ohio. Unlike those who advocated continued military resistance, he believed that their only chance of survival now lay in accommodation and adjustment, not in armed conflict. The majority of Shawnees who remained in Ohio followed his lead and tried to rebuild their lives around the new way of life offered by the United States. In the winter of 1802–03, Black Hoof traveled to Washington with a delegation of Shawnees and Delawares to help chart a new course for his people. He also visited the Quakers in Philadelphia. As a younger man he had gone among the Americans looking for scalps; now as an old man he went to them to ask for cattle, farm implements, and tools, and for help in building farms, sawmills, and gristmills. Jefferson furnished the delegates with a letter, via the secretary of war (at this time control of Indian affairs was still lodged in the War Department; it was moved to the Department of the Interior in 1849 and remains there today):

> Your father, the President, instructs me to assure you on behalf of your nation, that he will pay the most sacred regard to existing treaties between your respective nations and ours, and protect your whole territory against all intrusions that may be attempted

by white people. That all encouragement shall be given you in your just pursuits and laudable progress toward comfort and happiness, by the introduction of useful arts. That all persons, who shall offend against your treaties, shall be brought to justice, or if this should be impossible, that a faithful remuneration shall be made to you, and that he will never abandon his beloved Delawares and Shawnees, nor their children, so long as they shall act justly toward the white people and their red brethren.[6]

Meanwhile, in February, Jefferson wrote in private to the governor of Indiana Territory, William Henry Harrison, advising him to encourage Indians to run up debts at trading posts and then compel them to settle the bill by selling tribal lands. Ignoring the fact that Indian women in the eastern woodlands had been farming for hundreds of years, Jefferson and his contemporaries insisted on turning Indian men into farmers—farmers needed less land than hunters. Jefferson held out the promise that Indian people who became "civilized" could assimilate into American society, but he pursued policies that ensured their exclusion and removal.[7] The president sent the Shawnees some farm implements, but the Quakers did more than the government in trying to turn the Shawnees into yeoman farmers, the model citizens of Jefferson's agrarian republic.

Black Hoof's change of heart was not motivated by a newfound love of Americans and the way of life they offered.[8] Like many of the Cherokees who were also embracing American ways at this time, he thought it was the best available strategy for holding on to what was left of the homeland— perhaps the Americans would leave Indians alone if they saw them living like Americans. Black Hoof even asked the secretary of war for a deed defining the Shawnees' remaining lands in western Ohio. The government gave assurances of assistance and goodwill, but no deed.

Black Hoof also saw the new path as a way to outdo potential rivals for leadership of the Shawnees. As chief of the Mekoches, he resented the growing influence of the Kispoko brothers, Tecumseh and Tenskwatawa. They adopted a strongly anti-American stance and were in communication with the British. Black Hoof had had too much experience with British perfidy to go that route again. Instead, by cultivating relations with the United States he could bolster his position as legitimate chief of the Shawnees, position himself to obtain and distribute American supplies, and isolate his rivals.[9] To Black Hoof and the Americans, Tecumseh and his small band were recalcitrant troublemakers; to Tecumseh and his followers, Black Hoof and the older generations of chiefs had sold out and were pliant tools of the United States.

Early in 1807, Black Hoof traveled to Washington a second time, asking again for agricultural assistance. In response, the government authorized Baltimore Quaker William Kirk to set up a mission and a model farm at Wapakoneta. Kirk had first established a mission at Fort Wayne, working with Miamis and Potawatomis, but the Indian agent there, William Wells, wanted to monopolize the conduct of Indian affairs and undermined Kirk's efforts. Wells was an interesting character. Captured and adopted as a boy, he had grown up among the Miamis and had married the daughter of Little Turtle. He accompanied his Indian relatives on raids against white settlements, helped lure travelers on the Ohio River into ambush, and fought in the battles against Harmar and St. Clair. But he left his adopted family before the Battle of Fallen Timbers, enlisted as a scout in Wayne's army, and served as principal interpreter at Greenville. After the treaty, Wells continued to function as a culture broker between Indians and Americans. Like Black Hoof, his father-in-law Little Turtle was trying to follow the white man's path. There were those in both camps who harbored doubts about Wells's loyalty and integrity. In view of the life he lived, it is hardly surprising that Wells often played both ends and looked out for his own interests during his tenure as an Indian agent.[10]

Wapakoneta seemed to offer Kirk and his assistants better prospects. In June 1807, they left Fort Wayne and began the work of transforming the Shawnees. By the next spring, the Shawnees at Wapakoneta had planted more than five hundred acres, not only with the corn, beans, and squash their

women had cultivated for hundreds of years, but also with
potatoes, turnips, and cabbages. They used workhorses and
oxen to plow their fields. Their harvest in the fall was "boun-
teous." They had several small apple orchards and owned
some pigs and cattle. Some Shawnees continued to grow crops
in communal fields, in the traditional way; others fenced off
individual fields like the Americans. Kirk helped the community to hire a blacksmith, who began to operate a forge.
The Quakers also started building a gristmill and a sawmill.
Soon many Shawnees were living in log cabins with chimneys
and furniture, and dressed in white man's clothes. The Quaker
program involved far-reaching social changes as well as economic development. Relieved of the task of cultivating cornfields with hoes, Shawnee women could spend more time
attending to the kind of family and domestic tasks that
nineteenth-century Americans deemed appropriate for women:
milking cattle, spinning and weaving, washing clothes, cook-
ing. Shawnees were reluctant to have their children educated
in the white man's ways but eventually agreed to opening a
school. Black Hoof wrote to Jefferson thanking the government for sending the Quakers: "They are good people and
concerned for our welfare and have done a great deal for us in
instructing our young men in a good way and how to use the
tools we see in the hands of our white brothers."[11] Henry Harvey, a Quaker missionary, appreciated just how radical a step
the Wapakoneta Shawnees took "by adopting the life of their

oppressors" and exchanging "their Indian way of life for the life of a white man." Nevertheless, "these kind-hearted people had begun under the fostering care of the government, and by the aid of the Society, to realize better days." They could look forward to one day becoming "a prosperous and happy people."[12]

Unfortunately, Kirk got himself into financial difficulties by overspending and underreporting federal monies. He made himself an easy target for William Wells, who was angling to get control of the Shawnee annuities. He blew the whistle on Kirk, writing to Secretary of War Henry Dearborn that he was mismanaging funds and that the Shawnees were dissatisfied. Wells also seems to have helped spread rumors that Kirk was sleeping with Shawnee women. In December 1808, Wells traveled to Washington. While he was there, Dearborn dismissed Kirk. Black Hoof and other Shawnee chiefs wrote to Dearborn in protest. The bad stories that had been spread were false: "Since our friend Kirk has lived with us we have always found him a good man. We are very fond of him," they said. He had always given good advice and they wanted him back. It was to no avail. In April 1809, the Quakers abandoned their mission at Wapakoneta. The Shawnees presented Kirk with a parting gift of a belt of white wampum: "It is white and pure and will show you that our friendship is so too." William Wells's intrigues did him little good. A little more than a year after he secured Kirk's dismissal, Wells himself was dismissed as Indian agent.[13]

John Johnston took over as agent at Fort Wayne. With his assistance, Black Hoof and the Wapakoneta community continued to make progress on "the road to civilization." There were two areas where Black Hoof refused to compromise, however: He continued to hold Christian missionaries at arm's length and he tried to keep what was left of Shawnee lands out of American hands. Black Hoof had signed the Treaty of Greenville and he honored its terms. He signed additional treaties with the United States but none that took more Shawnee land, and he consistently made the case to the American government that the remaining Shawnee lands be protected. In this, Black Hoof saw eye to eye with his Kispoko rivals.

Most of the Shawnees living in Ohio in the first decade of the nineteenth century believed, no doubt reluctantly, that policies of accommodation rather than confrontation now offered the best chance for their survival and for holding on to their land. Like those Apache people who seventy years later believed that Geronimo and his band of holdouts were actually making things worse for the Apaches as a whole, Black Hoof and his followers feared Tenskwatawa and Tecumseh would jeopardize the progress they were making at Wapakoneta. At least that's what they told the Americans.

In fact, while Black Hoof and his followers made adjustments to American ways and on the surface appeared to walk a new road, they concealed a deeper conservatism and persistence of Shawnee ways. Missionaries saw this most clearly in their resistance to Christianity, but it was more than that. Thomas Jefferson and other American policymakers hoped that Indians who lived on reservations and received the appropriate instruction would be transformed into farmers and, in effect, cease to be Indians. Working in the fields instead of hunting in the woods dealt a blow to a Shawnee man's masculinity and identity, as it was intended to do, but in essential ways the Shawnees at Wapakoneta insisted on remaining Shawnee. Forced to give up land and compelled to live on it in different ways than their ancestors had done, they did not totally surrender to the invaders' vision of America. Shawnee women remained active in the new Shawnee agriculture. Shawnee men took up the plow but not the individual capitalism that was becoming the core value of nineteenth-century America. In the moral economy of a Shawnee community, sharing and taking care of relatives continued to outweigh individual ambition and the accumulation of property. As happened across America in the nineteenth century, Indian reservations that were designed to change the Indians forever became cultural refuges, places where Indian ways persisted and Indian communal values survived. In American eyes, such values were obstacles to progress and doomed Indians to perpetual backwardness. Indians would never "get ahead," they complained, so long as they squandered their wealth by giving it away. Despite the efforts to change them completely, reservation communities like Wapakoneta remained islands of Indianness within a sea of white American life.

Nevertheless, there were those who opposed Black Hoof, more militant voices that espoused a vision of Shawnee survival that had little place for Americans and that denounced the Wapakoneta way of dealing with them. In the summer of 1809, the United States perpetrated a land grab that played into the hands of Black Hoof's rivals.

7

THE VISIONS OF TENSKWATAWA AND TECUMSEH

WHEN BLACK HOOF signed the Treaty of Greenville, Tecumseh and Tenskwatawa moved west and took up residence alongside villages of refugee Delawares in Indiana.[1] While Black Hoof and his followers adjusted to a new way of life at Wapakoneta, Tenskwatawa offered a vision of the future built on an older understanding of what it meant to be Indian. While Black Hoof cultivated his garden and tried to hold on to what was left of the Shawnee homeland, Tecumseh cultivated an Indian confederation that would protect the lands and independence of all Indian people.

To some, Tecumseh is simply the greatest Indian who ever lived. He failed to achieve his goals, but his dream of a pan-Indian coalition has inspired generations of Native Americans.

In his prowess as a warrior, his generosity, and his concern for those who were older, younger, or weaker, Tecumseh epitomized the values that Shawnee society esteemed. His determination to stand his ground and the humanity he showed in war won admiration even from his enemies. His character, charisma, and courage made him a heroic figure in Canada and Europe as well as the United States.

Much apocrypha and many legends grew up after his death, but his contemporaries recognized that Tecumseh was a remarkable man. "There was a certain something in his countenance and manner that always commanded respect, and at the same time made those about him love him," recalled Stephen Ruddell, an adopted captive who grew up with him. Ruddell might be expected to have fond memories of the friend of his youth, but others shared his sentiments. Even William Henry Harrison, Tecumseh's nemesis, bestowed grudging praise. Tecumseh, he said, was "described by all as a bold, active sensible man, daring in the extreme, and capable of any undertaking." His followers were devoted to him. He was "one of those uncommon geniuses which spring up occasionally to produce revolutions and overturn the established order of things." Had it not been for the presence of the United States, Harrison reckoned, Tecumseh "would, perhaps, be the founder of an empire that would rival in glory that of Mexico or Peru."[2] Indian agent John Johnston said much the same thing. In his opinion, Tecumseh was "undoubtedly among the great men of his race." Had he appeared fifty years earlier his projected union of the tribes "might have set bounds to the Anglo-Saxon race in the West."[3]

Born around 1768, the year the Treaty of Fort Stanwix opened Shawnee hunting territories in Kentucky to invasion, Tecumseh inherited Kispoko divisional identity and membership in the panther clan from his father. His name has been interpreted as meaning Shooting Star or Crouching Panther, but the variants are probably not as far apart as might seem: The name probably refers to a celestial panther thought to be the spiritual protector of Tecumseh's clan, a starry creature that leaped across the skies.[4]

Tecumseh's father, Puckeshinwa, was killed at Point Pleasant. Two older brothers, Chisekau and Sauwauseekau, died fighting the Americans. As a boy, Tecumseh fled with his family as Big Knives burned Shawnee homes and crops. He fought at Fallen Timbers and he stayed away from the Treaty of Greenville. John Johnston said Tecumseh's hatred of whites was so deep-rooted "that he often said he never looked upon the face of a white man without being horror struck or feeling his flesh creep."[5]

However deep-seated his antipathy, Tecumseh did not succumb to blind hatred. His greatness lay in his humanity and his vision of a different future for Indian people. Ironically, in developing and pursuing that vision, Tecumseh owed

Tecumtha, or Tecumseh. Portrait from Benson J. Lossing, The Pictorial Field-Book of the War of 1812 *(1868), based on a sketch made by a trader at Vincennes during the War of 1812. Dartmouth College Library.*

much to his younger brother Lalawethika, described by Johnston as "a man devoid of talent or merit, a brawling mischievous Indian demagogue."[6]

It was Lalawethika, a singularly unattractive fellow by all accounts, who first came to prominence as the head of the movement that became Tecumseh's life work. Wounded as a youth in the right eye by an arrow that left him disfigured, and growing up in the shadow of older brothers who excelled in war and hunting, Lalawethika had a reputation as a hard-drinking loudmouth. His name meant "Rattler." He seemed to embody the evils that plagued the Shawnees and their neighbors at the turn of the century: alcoholism, poverty, disease, broken lives, dysfunctional and divided communities, loss of self-esteem, and lack of direction in a world of bewildering change and alien values.

Then, in the spring of 1805, Lalawethika fell into a trance. When he came to, he had quite a story to tell. He had crossed over into the spirit world where the Master of Life had shown him the past and the future and the torments that awaited Indian people who continued to live sinful lives. The experience made him a new man. He renounced his life of debauchery and gave up drinking. He experienced additional visions and took a new name: Tenskwatawa, "the Open Door." He preached that the Master of Life had chosen him to spread a new religion among the Indians. They were to return to their old ways and traditional values and renounce the things that had made them weak and corrupt. Indian people might continue to deal with the British, French, and Spaniards, but they must avoid contact with Americans. "The Americans I did not make," the Master of Life had told him. "They are not my children, but the children of the Evil Spirit. They are numerous but I hate them. They are unjust. They have taken away your lands, which were not made for them."[7] Indians must live like Indians if they were to recover their former strength and rebuild their world. They must abstain from alcohol, reject Christianity, cast off the white man's clothing, and stop using his tools. They should return to a diet of corn, beans, maple sugar, and deer meat and refuse to eat bread or the meat of domesticated animals. They could keep their guns for self-defense but must hunt with bows and arrows. They should practice communal ownership of property and reject the individual accumulation of wealth the Americans pursued. Indians should not resort to violence against Indians, whether tribes against tribes or husbands against wives. They should not be promiscuous but have monogamous marriages. They should pray morning and evening to the Master of Life, using prayer sticks Tenskwatawa provided, and they should throw away their medicine bundles that, like their shamans, had failed them in their time of need.

Tenskwatawa began to win disciples. He led a band of followers to Greenville in western Ohio and established a new village. With a 150-foot-long council house and fifty-seven

*Tenskwatawa, the Shawnee Prophet. One of several portraits done of
Tenskwatawa, this one was painted by Charles Bird King. Engraving
from Thomas L. McKenney and James Hall,* The Indian Tribes of
North America *(1836–44). Dartmouth College Library.*

smaller houses, Greenville became "a vital spiritual center."[8] Delawares, Kickapoos, Potawatomis, Ojibwas, Ottawas, Wyandots, Miamis, and Sauks came to hear the Prophet's teachings. Tenskwatawa even went to Wapakoneta to try to convince Black Hoof's people of the error of their ways.

Revitalization movements were not a new phenomenon in Indian country. From early contacts, whites had sometimes identified "prophets" who spurred Indians on to resistance, even if they did not fully comprehend their influence or what was happening in Indian communities. Such spirited resistance increased in reach and frequency as the crises facing Indian peoples intensified in the second half of the eighteenth century. A Delaware prophet, Neolin, had provided spiritual motivation for the movement that culminated in Pontiac's war against the British in 1763. As often happens, communities in crisis blamed outsiders as the cause of their misfortunes but looked within for the means of their salvation. Tenskwatawa's message drew on long-standing beliefs that associating with white men and their ways contaminated and diminished Native sources of sacred power; disassociating themselves was necessary to restore that power.[9]

Ominously, Tenskwatawa warned that those who opposed him opposed the wishes of the Master of Life and were likely to be guilty of witchcraft. Some of his disciples were quick to identify witches in their own communities, particularly among the older chiefs who had sold tribal lands to the

Americans. A brief but vicious witch hunt erupted among the Delawares, who executed a chief named Tetepachsit and several other people. Wyandot followers also executed several opponents of the Prophet's teachings whom they identified as witches. Many Indians rejected Tenskwatawa's teachings, but the United States played into his hands. Governor William Harrison of Indiana Territory denounced him as an impostor: If he was really a prophet, Harrison challenged, let him perform some kind of miracle, such as making the sun stand still or altering the course of the moon. Tenskwatawa, who likely knew that several teams of astronomers were in the Midwest getting ready for an upcoming eclipse, rose to the challenge and accurately predicted the total eclipse of the sun on June 16, 1806. His reputation soared. Meanwhile, the United States continued its assault on Indian lands and cultures, the very policies guaranteed to push frustrated young warriors into the Shawnee Prophet's camp. Even the aging Blue Jacket joined the Tecumseh-Tenskwatawa faction.

Three Shaker missionaries who visited the Prophet's village thought his movement had much in common with Christian religious awakenings. They told the Prophet: "Brother, we believe that the same good spirit is working in you & in us, which has told us how to put away all wicked ways & be a good people."[10] But many Americans were alarmed: Tenskwatawa's movement might turn violent, and the British in Canada would be only too happy to exploit the situation. Dur-

ing its war against Napoleonic France, the Royal Navy block-
aded European ports, stopped and searched American ships,
and removed American sailors suspected of desertion from
the British navy. Tensions escalated and threatened to produce a war between two countries whose wounds had not yet
healed after the Revolution. In 1807, a British warship search-
ing for deserters from the Royal Navy fired on an American
frigate. War seemed imminent.

That summer, while he was busy undermining Kirk's
position at Wapakoneta, William Wells started bombarding
the secretary of war with reports of Tenskwatawa's growing
influence and hostile intentions. "No thing can prevent the
assembling of the Indians at Greenvill[e] but the driving of
the Shawnese prophet as he is Called and his band from that
place which can not be done with words." "The Indians are
religiously *mad* and beleaves all the Shawnese says to them."
How long will "this fellow" be allowed to cause such trouble?
"He Deifies the United States to interrupt him and makes the
Indians beleave that if the government moves him from
Greenvill[e] there will be an end to the world." When the secretary of war criticized Wells's conduct and misuse of funds,
Wells became more strident. The "Shawnese Impostor" was
now a British agent poisoning the Indians against the United
States; he had to be stopped before he brought about an In-
dian war. Wells claimed to be doing everything he could to
prevent it; indeed, his lavish expenditure on gifts was the only

thing keeping all the Indians from going over to the Prophet and the British.[11] William Henry Harrison was equally convinced that Tenskwatawa was a British tool if not a British agent and that the Shawnees were inciting an Indian uprising. "War belts have been passing through all the Tribes from the Gulf of Florida to the lakes," the governor wrote in July 1807. "The Shawnees are the bearers of these belts and they have never been our friends."[12]

In fact, British dealings with the Indians were somewhat ambivalent. Britain expected the United States to attack Canada if war broke out but, distracted by the European conflict, could spare few troops to withstand an invasion. Once again, the British tried to restrain the Indians from actually starting a war but at the same time prepared them to rally to the defense of Canada if and when war broke out.

Governor Thomas Kirker of Ohio dispatched two commissioners to Greenville, with Stephen Ruddell as interpreter, to ascertain the Prophet's intentions. Blue Jacket assured the commissioners the Indians had no plans to join the British— after all, the redcoats had left them in the lurch in 1783 and 1794. Tenskwatawa accused Black Hoof and the Wapakoneta Shawnees of spreading lies. In September, Tecumseh, Blue Jacket, and the Wyandot chief Roundhead traveled to the state capital. They assured the governor of their pacific intentions but made it clear they intended to hold on to their lands. Although William Henry Harrison and others believed Tenskwatawa was a British pawn, the movement that was gathering momentum was driven by Indian grievances and goals, not by British strategy. Late in 1807, Main Poc, a Potawatomi war chief and shaman notable for his withered hand and his physical and spiritual powers, allied himself to the movement. Main Poc suggested that Tenskwatawa move west to Potawatomi land. The next spring Tenskwatawa established a new village near the junction of the Wabash and Tippecanoe Rivers. Indians gravitated to the new site in growing numbers. Americans called it Prophetstown. Between 1808 and 1811, the Prophet's followers increased from no more than one hundred to almost one thousand.[13] True to form, the Americans proved to be the movement's best recruitment officers.

In the summer of 1809, Governor Harrison assembled a group of compliant chiefs from the Delawares, Miamis, and Potawatomis at Fort Wayne. No Shawnees participated, but Little Turtle, the former Miami war chief, was there, as was a Potawatomi chief named Winamac. In return for $5,250 in trade goods and increased annual subsidies, the chiefs ceded more than three million acres of land in Illinois and Indiana.[14] Outraged by the size of the cession and the way the deal was done, Indians throughout the Midwest recoiled from the government chiefs—"whiskey chiefs," they called them. They turned instead to Tenskwatawa and Tecumseh.

The Shawnee brothers denounced the Fort Wayne treaty. The ceded lands belonged to all Indians, they said, not just to the tribes that sold them. Shawnees had fought to protect Shawnee land, but united defense of all tribal lands was not a new idea. The northwest confederacy had adopted the same stance in the 1780s and 1790s. As a young man Tecumseh had fought in Blue Jacket's confederacy. Blue Jacket died around 1808, but Tecumseh drew from his example. He sought to revive and extend that confederacy, and channeled his brother's religious movement into a militant defense of Indian lands and independence. The outrage at Fort Wayne pushed him and his movement along. Messengers from Prophetstown fanned out across Indian country, and Tecumseh himself began to travel among the tribes, winning converts to the cause with fiery oratory. Before 1809, Tecumseh seems to have stood behind Tenskwatawa—sources referred to him as "the brother of the Prophet." Now he stepped forward to lead the movement. In the words of Tecumseh's biographer John Sugden, the Treaty of Fort Wayne "put Tecumseh on the road to war."[15]

Tecumseh's movement was a coalition of warriors, not of tribes. Only a minority of the Shawnees followed him, those who preferred to continue the struggle rather than accept the kind of half-life that Black Hoof and his people seemed to endure at Wapakoneta. Like militant young Arabs who prefer to die fighting rather than live under corrupt rulers they regard as American puppets, warriors from far and wide cast aside their venal chiefs and gravitated to Tecumseh and his vision of a still-strong Indian nation that would stand up to American aggression.

In August 1810, Tecumseh met with Harrison at Vincennes, confronting the enemy face to face. In a council held in a clearing near the governor's residence at Grouseland, Tecumseh recited a litany of injustices Indians had suffered at American hands. He forcefully stated his position that the lands belonged to all and were not to be gobbled up piecemeal in illegal treaties with individual tribes. He demanded that the Treaty of Fort Wayne be rescinded and pointed angrily at Winamac, who sat near Harrison nervously clutching a brace of pistols. Harrison countered that the lands had been bought and paid for. Tempers frayed and at one point Tecumseh called Harrison a liar. Warriors grabbed their tomahawks and soldiers hurried to arms. For a moment a bloodbath seemed imminent. But the parties adjourned, cooled down, and reconvened the next day.

The negotiations continued on and off for more than a week, but there was no meeting of minds or common ground. Harrison invited the Shawnee brothers to visit the president in Washington, but Tecumseh declined. He warned Harrison to make no more treaties with village chiefs because he, Tecumseh, was now "the acknowledged chief of all the Indians." The prospect of a pan-Indian movement with Tecumseh at its head was alarming to Harrison and the United States, whose policies depended on dividing and dispossessing the tribes.

Harrison said he would convey Tecumseh's demands to Washington but doubted the president would agree to them. Tecumseh said he hoped the Great Spirit would "put some sense" into the president's head and induce him to return the Indians' land. Otherwise, "He may sit still in his town, and drink his wine, while you and I will have to fight it out."[16]

In November, Tecumseh went to Amherstburg with a delegation of 160 followers. Located on the Canadian side of the Detroit River, Amherstburg was the hub of British-Indian relations, and Matthew Elliott was now superintendent of Indian affairs. Tecumseh had been there a couple of years before to sound out the British, but now he told Elliott his confederacy was ready for action. The old chiefs had been ruining their country, but "we the Warriors now manage the Affairs of our Nation." "You Father, have nourished and raised us up from Childhood, we are now Men, and think ourselves capable of defending our Country." They were determined to defend themselves and expected the British to assist them with supplies.[17]

For several years, Elliott had been handing out supplies. No doubt he handed out more words of advice than ever made it into the written records, as the British Indian department tried to keep the Indians in readiness for the anticipated war with the United States. Elliott had lived with the Shawnees, devoted much of his life to bolstering the Shawnee resistance, and sometimes, said his critics, let his

Shawnee attachments and sympathies affect his judgment. Like Alexander McKee, he maintained connections through his Shawnee relatives. Illiterate himself, Elliott was assisted by a clerk and storekeeper, George Ironside, who had been educated at King's College, Aberdeen. Like McKee and Elliott, Ironside had also been a trader in Shawnee country and lived with a Shawnee woman. A British army captain who was hostile to Elliott said he had no influence except with the Shawnees, but influence with the Shawnees usually translated into influence with other Indians. The captain complained that all the officers in the Indian department were "indeed in some way connected with this tribe either by Marriage or Concubinage which occasions that partiality so manifest in their favor, & which has been evidently the cause of that nation having been always more insolent and troublesome than any other."[18] A spiteful officer anxious to discredit Elliott overstated the situation, but Tecumseh had good reason to expect that Elliott's Indian department would assist a Shawnee war chief and his confederacy.

Tecumseh left Amherstburg and headed deep into Indian country. He carried his message of pan-Indian land tenure and preached his vision of a united Indian nation from Canada to the Gulf of Mexico. He visited the Shawnees and Wyandots in Ohio, went on to the tribes in Michigan, dispatched messengers to the Iroquois in New York, traveled west to the Illinois and Mississippi, and tried to enlist the

Shawnees living in Missouri. "You see him today on the Wabash and in a short time you hear of him on the shores of Lake Erie or Michigan, or on the banks of the Mississippi," Harrison wrote, "and wherever he goes he makes an impression favorable to his purposes."[19] A white captive who heard Tecumseh speak to the Osages said he could not find the words "to do justice to the eloquence of this distinguished man," but the speech "made an impression on my mind, which, I think, will last as long as I live."[20]

Tecumseh met with Harrison again at Vincennes in July 1811, assuring him that the confederacy he was building wanted peace, not war. Then he departed for the South. John Norton heard of Tecumseh during his travels in Cherokee country, although he usually referred to him as the brother of the Prophet. He said he was known as "a very sensible man, and brave Warrior, of an independent spirit, and enthusiastic to preserve the territory and independence of his brethren." He insisted "that the right the Great Spirit had given the Aboriginal Natives to the soil they possess, should be defended even at the expence of their lives."[21]

Tecumseh and a delegation of Shawnees, Kickapoos, and Winnebagos traveled to the Chickasaws, Choctaws, and Creeks, nations that, along with the Cherokees and Seminoles, the United States designated the "Civilized Tribes" on account of the headway they had made in adjusting to Anglo-American ways of life. Dominated by the mixed-blood leadership of the Colbert family, the Chickasaws were not receptive to Tecumseh's teachings. Among the Choctaws, one of the largest nations in the South, the influential chief Pushmataha spoke against Tecumseh. But in Creek country there were many who listened. The Shawnees had long-standing connections and relatives there, and Creek communities were already divided over the question of American "civilization." The fact that a comet appeared in the night skies that fall at the same time that Tecumseh—the Shooting Star—was there made a striking impression on many Creeks. They were even more impressed when, shortly after Tecumseh left, an earthquake struck. The effects of the New Madrid earthquakes, a series of shocks lasting from mid-December 1811 to early February, were felt across the South. For a while, the Mississippi flowed backward, and the town of New Madrid was destroyed. The story grew up that Tecumseh had predicted the quakes, telling the Creeks that when he got back to Detroit he would stamp his foot and make the earth tremble. Whatever its sources, Tecumseh left his mark in Creek country and fueled a growing discontent that soon exploded in revolt and civil war.

Tecumseh was home before the tremors subsided, but he was in for a different kind of shock. When he returned to the Wabash he found Prophetstown in ruins and many of his followers scattered.

During his absence, William Henry Harrison led a

preemptive strike against Prophetstown. The Prophet's warriors monitored the advance of the American army up the Wabash, and Tenskwatawa assured them that the Master of Life had given him medicine to defeat the Long Knives. He told them they would be invulnerable to American bullets and invisible to American eyes in the darkness. A couple of hours before dawn on November 7, 1811, Indians began to encircle Harrison's camp and infiltrate his lines. A sentry fired a shot in alarm and the Indians launched their attack. Some hurled themselves against the soldiers as they tried to scramble to their defensive positions; others, firing from the darkness, shot down soldiers illuminated by their own campfires. It seemed the Prophet's medicine was working. As the Americans fell back from the fury of the attack, it looked for a moment as if Harrison might experience the kind of defeat St. Clair had suffered. But the American lines held, and as day broke it became clear that the Indians had neither the numbers nor the ammunition to sustain a long fight with almost one thousand well-equipped troops. A bayonet charge finally drove the Indians from the field.

Harrison claimed the Battle of Tippecanoe was a decisive victory; indeed, in 1840 he and his running mate, John Tyler, won the presidency on the slogan "Tippecanoe and Tyler too." But the battle was a close call and a pyrrhic victory. The Americans suffered 188 casualties. The Indians, who were outnumbered as much as two to one and attacking a defensive position, lost perhaps fifty killed and as many wounded. Tecumseh dismissed the battle as a "scuffle between children."

But Tecumseh was trying to make the best of a bad situation. Tippecanoe was a major reverse for the confederacy. Some of the warriors retreating from the battlefield turned on Tenskwatawa as a false prophet and then headed home to their own villages. Prophetstown was abandoned and the Americans burned it. According to some reports, Tecumseh was so angry with his brother he shook him by the hair. The Indians faced a hard winter after the Americans burned stores and crops. Tecumseh faced a formidable task in rebuilding the confederacy. He dispatched runners to bring back his disgruntled followers. "It is better to die as men at once than die a lingering death," Shawnee messages said.[22]

Tecumseh also looked to Canada for assistance. The British were finally ready to enter the fray. On June 18, 1812, the United States declared war on Britain. War hawks in the United States clamored for an invasion of Canada; only by making common cause with Tecumseh's confederacy did the British have any hope of defending it. The Prophet told the Americans that the British had invited the Indians to take up arms against the United States. Tecumseh led his warriors north.

Not all Shawnees followed him. Most Ohio Shawnees followed the lead of Black Hoof and remained neutral or even supported the Americans. When the war broke out, Black

Hoof and several other chiefs—Captain Lewis, Logan, and the Wolf—scouted for American armies. They tried to dissuade warriors from joining the British and reminded them of how Britain had treated its Indian allies in the past, urging them on to war and then abandoning them to their fate. Black Hoof said the British "viewed the Indians as they did their dogs. That when they told them to bite, they must bite." But the Shawnees were not dogs; they were men and "would make their own decisions."[23] Black Hoof's decision almost cost him his life. Americans remained suspicious of the Shawnees at Wapakoneta, and while he was acting as a scout a would-be assassin in the American militia took a shot at him. The bullet entered his left cheek and lodged in his right cheekbone. Black Hoof recovered from the wound but yet again Americans had attempted to kill one of their best friends in Indian country.[24]

When the war started, General William Hull was at Detroit, poised to invade Canada. He crossed the Detroit River on July 12, easily sweeping aside what puny opposition the British and Canadians could mount, and moved on the British post at Fort Malden. But things did not go as the Americans anticipated. Hull lost his nerve and lost the initiative to Tecumseh, who rallied his warriors. Meanwhile a force of British and Indians captured the strategic Fort Michilimackinac at the straits between Lake Michigan and Lake Huron, inspiring many northern tribes to join the British-Indian alliance. Then Potawatomis captured Fort Dearborn, the site of modern-day Chicago, and killed most of the garrison as they evacuated. William Wells led the garrison and their families out of the fort. The former captive turned Miami turned U.S. Indian agent painted his face black in expectation of death. Potawatomi warriors killed him and ate his heart to ingest his courage. That was August 15. The next day, Tecumseh and the British took Detroit.

Tecumseh and his Wyandot ally Roundhead ambushed a superior American force at Brownstown, south of Detroit, and clashed with the Americans again at Monguagon, threatening Hull's supply lines. Captured mail revealed that the general magnified in his mind the number of Indians he faced. Hull pulled his demoralized army back to Detroit. When British reinforcements led by General Isaac Brock arrived from the Niagara region, Tecumseh and the British went on the offensive.

The brief but brilliant alliance between Tecumseh and Brock has become part of the lore of the War of 1812 in Canada. Unlike Hull, both men were courageous and decisive leaders. Almost immediately they developed mutual respect and an effective working relationship. Playing on Hull's fears by making sure he saw plenty of Indians, they attacked Detroit. Fearing for the safety of his noncombatants, Hull surrendered almost immediately, to the chagrin and humiliation of his men. Tecumseh's dream of a united Indian resistance ably supported by redcoat allies and of stopping the American advance in its tracks was becoming a reality.

But it was not to be. Brock was killed at the Battle of Queenston Heights on the Niagara frontier in October. No one else in the British military enjoyed similar standing with the Indians. Colonel Henry Proctor, a man of different mettle, assumed command. The British and the Indians continued to win victories, but their war effort lost momentum. Kentucky militia burned Indian villages on the Wabash and American armies advanced to avenge the humiliation at Detroit.

The Wyandot chief Roundhead and Proctor defeated General James Winchester's force of Kentuckians at the River Raisin in January 1813, a victory marred by the Indian slaughter of some American wounded and prisoners. In May, as they lay siege to William Henry Harrison's army at Fort Meigs, Tecumseh and the British scored another victory, routing a Kentuckian relief column. After the battle, Indian warriors again began to kill their prisoners. When Tecumseh heard what was happening he rode to the scene and put a stop to it. Brandishing his tomahawk, he denounced the warriors as cowards and denounced British officers for failing to prevent the killings. About forty Americans died but Tecumseh's action at Fort Meigs, perhaps more than any other, won him the respect of contemporaries and the admiration of subsequent generations. With a victory under their belt, however, many of the Indian warriors dispersed, compelling Tecumseh and

Proctor to raise the siege and take up defensive positions in Canada.

The British forces in Upper Canada lay at the far end of a precarious supply line by water that stretched a thousand miles from Montreal and was frozen and impassable much of the year. Supplies were badly needed for the war in the East and few could be spared for the war in the West. Tecumseh struggled to keep his Indian army assembled when they needed to be off hunting or returning to their homes and families, and relations became strained as the British failed to provide the material support they had promised.

In September 1813, Captain Oliver H. Perry defeated Captain Robert Barclay's little British fleet on Lake Erie. The Americans could now sever Proctor's supply lines and land troops in his rear. As Harrison's army advanced, Proctor had little choice but to retreat from Fort Malden, but he failed to communicate his reasons or his strategy to his senior officers or to the Indians. When he saw the redcoats making preparations to pull out, Tecumseh rounded on Proctor. He reminded the general how the British had betrayed the Indians after the Revolution and after the Battle of Fallen Timbers. When war broke out in 1812, the British handed them the tomahawk and promised to help them get their lands back. Now the Indians saw the British getting ready to abandon the fort and feared another betrayal. They knew the fleet had fought but did not yet know the outcome and did not know what Proctor's intentions were. "We must compare our Father's conduct to a fat Animal that carries its tail upon its back; but when affrighted, it drops it between its legs and runs off," Tecumseh scolded. If the British wanted to run away, they were welcome to go, but they should at least leave arms and ammunition for the Indians to use. "Our lives are in the hands of the Great Spirit," he concluded. "We are determined to defend our lands, and if it is his Will, we wish to leave our bones upon them."[25]

Proctor finally explained the necessity for a retreat to the Thames River in Ontario and Tecumseh acceded to it. The army burned Fort Malden and abandoned Amherstburg. Matthew Elliott and Simon Girty left their homes, and the Americans destroyed them. Elliott by this time was about seventy-five years old, with white flowing hair. Girty was almost blind. Proctor was thinking in terms of a broader strategy, but most of the Indians were more concerned with defending their lands and families. Many refused to withdraw from the Detroit region and began to leave the army. Main Poc led a group to Michigan. Roundhead, Tecumseh's steadfast ally, died of natural causes. The Indians who retreated with the British included many women and children. They had little confidence in Proctor and, by this time, neither did his troops. Angry warriors threatened Elliott's life during the retreat, and the old man was reduced to tears at the state of affairs.[26]

General Harrison pursued with an army of more than

three thousand regulars and militia. By the time the British finally turned to make a stand, near the Indian village of Moraviantown on the Thames River, Proctor had abandoned most of his artillery and squandered the confidence of his men. Eyewitnesses said that Tecumseh had a premonition of death the night before the battle. The next afternoon, Harrison's army attacked. Heavily outnumbered and sensing the hopelessness of their situation, the British troops fired only a couple of volleys before they broke. Six hundred surrendered to the Americans. Matthew Elliott called their conduct "shameful in the highest degree." Proctor himself fled the field and was later court-martialed.[27]

The only effective resistance came from Tecumseh and the Indians on the right wing. Rallying his warriors even as his hopes for an independent Indian future evaporated, Tecumseh was shot down in the midst of bitter hand-to-hand fighting. According to various reports, the body of the man who had stopped the killing of American prisoners at Fort Meigs was scalped and mutilated. Some said the Americans skinned his corpse. The mutilation of Indian bodies on the battlefield frustrated American efforts to identify Tecumseh and gave rise to generations of mystery and controversy about the Shawnee leader's final resting place.[28]

Tenskwatawa tried to rally Indian support but Tenskwatawa was no Tecumseh. Indians continued to fight in the War of 1812, but it was little more than a holding action as the war wound down. In the South, the Indian movement that Te-cumseh had helped to inspire met disaster. Prophets among the Red Stick Upper Creeks echoed the message of Tenskwa-tawa and Tecumseh, preaching rejection of American influ-ences and resistance to American expansion.

But the Creek confederacy, a loose coalition of many au-tonomous towns, was divided, and tensions erupted in civil war. The Creek War began and ended in carnage. In August 1813, Red Stick warriors attacked and destroyed Fort Mims on the Alabama River, killing about 250 American men, women, and children, as well as Indians who had taken ref-uge there. The Red Sticks hoped to involve the British and the Spanish, and the British for a time planned a joint British-Indian strategy in the South, but in the end the Red Sticks fought alone. Spurred on by the Fort Mims massacre, the Americans quickly launched expeditions into Creek country. General Andrew Jackson of Tennessee inflicted a string of crushing defeats on the Red Sticks, culminating at the Battle of Horseshoe Bend, where, assisted by Cherokee and Creek allies, the Americans killed about eight hundred Red Stick warriors. Jackson had his men cut off the noses of the fallen Indians to tally the body count. At the Treaty of Fort Jack-son in August 1814, Jackson dictated peace terms and confis-cated almost two-thirds of the Creek homeland, including lands belonging to the Lower Creeks who had assisted him in the war.

During the negotiations held at Ghent in Belgium to end the War of 1812, the British for a time tried to honor their commitment to Tecumseh by arguing for an independent Indian state between Canada and the United States. But the Americans would have none of it, and the British had no intention of continuing the war for the Indians. They settled instead for a clause that restored the Indians to their "status quo antebellum," that is, to the situation that had existed before the war. The peace was signed on Christmas Eve, 1814. Weeks later, Andrew Jackson defeated a British army at New Orleans, a victory that boosted his reputation and the nation's morale but had no effect on the outcome of a war that had already ended.

Once again, Britain washed its hands of its Indian allies. The Americans did not return the lands confiscated by Andrew Jackson and, as the British Earl of Bathurst explained in response to Indian complaints about continued American encroachments, the Treaty of Ghent stipulated no more than that the United States should restore to the Indians the lands they held before the war. "It does not nor was it ever intended on the part of Great Britain to guarantee those territories and possessions against future Invasion after they had been restored."[29]

In years to come both Andrew Jackson and William Henry Harrison won the presidency with election campaigns that emphasized their victories over both the British and the

Indians. With the British and Indians defeated in the North and in the South, the United States was free to pursue unchecked national expansion. Indian resistance east of the Mississippi did not end—the Seminoles in Florida continued to resist, and a brief and brutal conflict known as Black Hawk's War erupted in Illinois in 1832. But Shawnees would never again take the lead in orchestrating a united Indian defense against the United States. The heartland of America was to be "American."

8

REMOVALS AND SURVIVALS

THE VISION OF a united and independent Indian state east of the Mississippi died with Tecumseh. Harrison had described Tecumseh as "the Moses" of the Indian movement and there was no one else to fill that role. But the war for survival took many forms. Black Hoof and others reasserted the strategy of retaining tribal homelands by cooperating with, rather than resisting, the United States, and reaffirmed their position as tribal leaders by functioning as government chiefs. After the War of 1812, American population pressure and United States policy combined to remove Indians west of the Mississippi, and many Americans regarded their expulsion as inevitable. But Black Hoof and the Ohio Shawnees worked to secure a future in Ohio by transforming their economy, tolerating missionaries, and dealing with the United States government.[1] Unfortunately, the steps Shawnees took along the path laid out for them by the United States government failed to preserve what remained of their lands. In the end, the United States treated former allies no better than former enemies.

In September 1817, U.S. commissioners held a treaty with the Wyandots, Senecas, Ojibwas, Ottawas, Potawatomis, and Shawnees at the foot of the rapids of the Miami. The treaty extinguished almost all remaining Indian title to lands in Ohio, except for ten miles square around Wapakoneta, twenty-five square miles at Hog Creek, and forty-eight square miles at Lewistown, where Shawnees and Senecas shared a reservation. The treaty made no provision for the Shawnees who had lived on the Wabash River and had followed Tecumseh. But the Shawnees at Wapakoneta, "in consideration of the faithful services of the Shawnees in the late war with England, and for divers other considerations," received an annuity of two thousand dollars, to be managed by the chiefs, and grants of land. The government also gave lands to Black Hoof and other chiefs at Wapakoneta and the chiefs residing at Hog Creek, and forty acres to Captain Lewis at the Lewistown reservation. Quaker missionary Henry Harvey said that of all the treaties made between the United States and the Shawnees, this was the only one he could find that had "the appearance of fairness," the first one that did not demand land from the Shawnees. Nevertheless, the

United States was clearly exerting its influence in Shawnee politics to strengthen the power of chiefs it regarded as pro-American.[2]

In 1819, according to Indian agent John Johnston, 800 Shawnees lived in Ohio. There were 559 at Wapakoneta, 72 at Hog Creek, ten miles to the north, and another 169 at Lewistown.[3] At Wapakoneta Black Hoof's people continued to walk a path of accommodation. But they still selected what they needed and rejected what they could not accept. They raised cattle and pigs to help offset the decline in hunting off their reservations.[4] The Quakers established another mission at Wapakoneta and sent missionary Henry Harvey, who later wrote a history of the Shawnees. The Quakers also opened a school. But, John Johnston wrote, they did not yet try to instruct the Shawnees in the principles of Christianity, believing that they were "not yet sufficiently acquainted with the arts of civilized life." They remained "bitterly opposed to Christianity," arguing that God had given Shawnees their own religion, just as he had given white people theirs.[5] More than half a century later, when Thomas Wildcat Alford and a friend were about to leave the Shawnee reservation in Oklahoma and attend the boarding school at Hampton Institute in Virginia, two of the more traditional chiefs solemnly reminded them that they were representing the Shawnee nation. They must learn the white man's ways so that they could return home and become chiefs, but *"we should not accept the white man's religion; we must remain true to the Shawnee faith"* (Alford's italics).[6]

Tenskwatawa tried to secure a leadership role in the developments that were taking place. While in Ontario he tried to make himself an important liaison with the British Indian department and he also negotiated with Governor Lewis Cass of Michigan. Cass, who had fought at Detroit and the Battle of the Thames, was emerging as a loud voice in Indian affairs and a leading advocate of Indian removal. He paid more attention to Tenskwatawa than did the British and even interviewed him about traditional Shawnee life and culture. The Prophet and his band moved to Michigan in 1824. Cass encouraged him to return to Ohio and use his influence there to induce his tribesmen to move west. Captain Lewis was also working for removal.[7]

In anticipation of removing the Shawnees, the federal government set up a new reservation in the West. Shawnees had been moving west since the late eighteenth century, forming settlements along Apple Creek near Cape Girardeau in Missouri and on the Merrimack River near St. Louis. Some Shawnees joined their relatives in Missouri soon after the War of 1812, and there were now about twelve hundred living in Missouri, considerably more than remained in Ohio.[8] Daniel Boone, who had played a key role in destroying the Shawnees' world in Kentucky, found the world that replaced it not much to his liking and led his family west to Missouri in 1799.

Quatawapea, or Captain Lewis, head of the Shawnees and Senecas at Lewistown. Painted by Charles Bird King during a visit to Washington in 1825. Engraving from Thomas L. McKenney and James Hall, The Indian Tribes of North America *(1836–44). Dartmouth College Library.*

There, during the last twenty years of his life, he renewed friendships and went hunting with Shawnees he had known in the East. Like him, they had migrated to Missouri to escape the press of American settlement.[9] But they soon felt the pressure there, too: "We are very much crowded by the whites, who steal our horses and many other things," Cape Girardeau Shawnees complained to Governor William Clark in 1815.[10]

Clark, who had traveled to the Pacific with Meriwether Lewis twenty years before and was now superintendent of Indian affairs, made a treaty with the Missouri Shawnees in November 1825. They gave up their twenty-five-mile-square tract of lands around Cape Girardeau in exchange for a fifty-mile-square tract in what is now eastern Kansas, which the United States had purchased from the Osages, or, if that proved unacceptable to them, an equal amount of land on the Kansas River. The government paid the Shawnees fourteen thousand dollars for their improvements.[11] The new reservation was to serve as the reservation for all Shawnees, whether from Missouri or Ohio.

Tenskwatawa led about 250 people from Wapakoneta in the fall of 1826. They endured a miserable winter, huddled in hastily constructed huts near Kaskaskia, Illinois, on the Mississippi. They spent the next winter on the Osage River in Missouri. They finally reached the new Shawnee reservation in eastern Kansas in spring of 1828.[12] Four years later, the artist George Catlin sought out Tenskwatawa and painted his portrait. Despite his claims to be a leader of his people, that was the most attention the Shawnee Prophet received after he had collaborated in moving Shawnees westward. He lived the rest of his life in obscurity, no doubt haunted by old dreams and perhaps a few demons.

Tenskwatawa was just one of 482 Shawnees who migrated from Ohio across the Mississippi before 1830. Captain Lewis led a band of Shawnees and Senecas from Lewistown in the mid-1820s, and other leaders such as Black Wolf, Logan, Big Snake, and Silverheels also took their people west. As they loaded their belongings and departed, they left behind things that suggest their material life was now not very different from that of their white neighbors: log houses, some with floors, fence rails, peach and apple trees, vegetable gardens, plows, hoes, kettles, frying pans. Some also left, or lost along the way, hogs, hens, horses, and milk cows. Black Hoof and some 286 Shawnees remained at Wapakoneta, but not for long. The era of voluntary migrations was over.[13]

Andrew Jackson was elected president in 1828. Jackson did not invent the policy of evicting eastern Indians from their homelands and relocating them beyond the Mississippi, but he did more than anyone else to see that it was implemented. In May 1830, Congress passed the Indian Removal Act, authorizing the president to negotiate treaties by which the tribes remaining in the East would exchange their lands for new territories set aside for them in the West. Despite vocal opposition from some quarters, the Jackson administration pushed forward relentlessly with the new policy. Shawnees who had gambled that living like Americans would allow them to live on Shawnee lands lost their bet.

Henry Harvey witnessed the unpleasant business of removing the Shawnees. Harvey took charge of the Society of Friends School for the Shawnees near Wapakoneta and moved there with his family. He found the Shawnees "an uncommonly pleasant and lively people" and was a severe critic of the treatment they received at the hands of professed Christians. From the time the Quakers first arrived to work with them, the Shawnees had expressed fear that improving their land would only make white people more eager to get their hands on it and that the government would drive them off. The Quakers had assured them that the United States government would not stoop so low as to break its solemn pledges to them and they would never have to give up their land. "Alas! What a mistake!" wrote Harvey. The Shawnees protested, and even Lewis Cass, who was now secretary of war, supported them, but President Jackson refused to hear their case.[14]

On July 20, 1831, the Shawnees and Senecas living at Lewistown, Ohio, signed a treaty, ceding their reservation in Ohio for sixty thousand acres in northeastern Oklahoma, to which they moved the next year. On August 8, the Shawnees at Wapakoneta and Hog Creek signed a treaty ceding their lands in Ohio in return for a hundred thousand acres within the reservation in eastern Kansas. Instead of compensating the Shawnees for the improvements they had made on their Ohio lands, the government promised to advance six thousand dollars to the Lewistown band and thirteen thousand dollars to the Wapakoneta and Hog Creek Shawnees. The advances and the cost of building a sawmill, gristmill, and blacksmith shop on the new reservations would be deducted from the sales of the Indians' Ohio lands and the balance would be used to fund annuities for the removed tribes.[15]

Black Hoof, whom Tenskwatawa and Tecumseh had vilified for selling out, refused to sign and never moved. He died early in 1832, without having relinquished any more land. Henry Harvey attended the funeral. The Shawnees buried their old chief "in the Indian manner," and the funeral was "conducted entirely after their ancient Indian style." Black Hoof had been their chief for more than thirty years and was "always an advocate for his own nation." His passing left the Shawnees in great straits at a critical time in their history and marked the end of an era.[16] No longer would the Shawnees be led by chiefs who had fought the Americans. A younger man, named John Perry, took over as leader of the Ohio Shawnees.[17]

Harvey saw firsthand the deceit and mismanagement that accompanied the Shawnees' removal. He blamed most of it on James B. Gardiner, an Ohio politician and Jackson supporter whom the secretary of war appointed special agent to the Ohio tribes and authorized to superintend their removal. The government investigated Gardiner's handling of the business, but the problem went much deeper than Gardiner and reached all the way to Washington. When Gardiner negotiated the removal treaties, he told the Shawnees they would be relocated to their new homes early in the spring. He advised them to sell their cattle, hogs, and other property they could not take with them and settle up their affairs. The proceeds from the sales, together with their annuity, would be paid to them when they started west in the spring. They did as he advised, sold about two hundred head of cattle and twelve hundred hogs, and bought clothing, wagons, guns, and provisions for the trip. Local merchants took advantage of the situation, "filching from them the last dollar for which they have sold their heritage amongst us, and the 'graves of their fathers,' " wrote Gardiner.

Expecting to move in the spring, they did not plant corn that year. But the Senate did not ratify the removal treaties until April 1832, and Congress did not appropriate funds for carrying them out until August. Instead of moving in the spring, they moved in the fall, and did not receive any money until then. They had used up all their provisions, had no money, and as they were about to leave the country, could not get credit. For several months they had little food. "I saw more real suffering during that time among the Shawnees, for food, than I had ever expected to witness in my whole life," wrote Harvey. Gardiner had told them they would be fairly compensated for their improvements, moved at government expense, and supported for one year after their arrival. Instead, said Harvey, they received less than half the value of their improvements and had to pay many of the costs of removal themselves. They received corn and meat for the first year but had to pay for the buildings and other accommodations made for them.[18]

Preparations for removal were held up; supplies were inadequate and arrived late. The Shawnees refused to travel by steamboat. They told Gardiner they had no wish "to move by fire," or be scalded "like the white man cleans his hog." They got their way.[19] In September, the Shawnees left Wapakoneta, the community they had built on the belief that Americans might yet be trusted. Henry Harvey watched them go. "They set off with heavy hearts on their journey of eight hundred miles across the open prairie." Many wept openly as they said farewell to their homes; some were in despair. Even if they managed to rebuild their lives in the new country, what was to stop the government from taking their lands from them again? Leaving late in the season, they were overtaken by winter during their trek west. They traveled in fear of disease and crossed the Mississippi above St. Louis to escape the cholera that was prevalent that year. But they could not escape the traders and whiskey peddlers who followed them like vultures. "I would to God I could say we were also away from those mean and miserable wretches," fumed Gardiner.[20]

The following summer the Shawnees at Hog Creek left, apart from a dozen families who refused to migrate because of sickness and who did not move to Kansas until 1838. Reviewing the Shawnees' experiences and the catalogue of broken promises made them, Harvey concluded: "How little regard was paid to the faith of our nation, or to the wants of these poor people."[21]

The Shawnees, whom Edmund Atkin had described as "the greatest travelers in America" in the East in the eighteenth century, continued their travels in the West in the nineteenth century. Some of the Shawnees who had migrated to Missouri went south and settled at different times in Arkansas, Louisiana, and, in company with groups of Cherokees, Delawares, Kickapoos, Quapaws, Choctaws, and Caddos, in eastern Texas, which was still part of Mexico. In 1822, after Mexico won its independence from Spain, a large band of Shawnees, numbering about 270 warriors, which would indicate well over a thousand people, settled south of the Red River and petitioned the Mexican authorities for land. The governor of Coahuila and Texas drew up a temporary contract in 1824, granting lands to each family. Delawares and other immigrant Indians joined them. They grew crops, raised cattle, and traded extensively. On occasion Shawnees clashed with, and held their own against, the powerful Comanches. They coexisted peacefully with the Mexicans, but they never received official title to their land.

After Texas won its independence from Mexico in 1836, the first president, Sam Houston, promised to grant the immigrant Indians title. But his successor Mirabeau Lamar believed Indians had no rights the new government of Texas needed to respect, and his administration pursued a relentless policy of cleansing Texas of its Indian populations.[22] In August 1839, the Shawnees made a treaty at Nacogdoches, agreeing to leave Texas if the government paid compensation and provided assistance. A few Shawnees remained, but most of the immigrant Indians moved north and settled on the Canadian River in Oklahoma. They formed the nucleus of the modern-day Absentee Shawnees, a designation first applied to those Shawnees who were not residing on the Shawnee reservation in Kansas when it was allotted in 1854.[23] The last Shawnees to leave Texas arrived in Oklahoma in 1859.

Shawnees in the West continued to fight and confederate. From the time they first arrived in Missouri, Shawnees joined with Delawares, Cherokees, and other emigrant tribes in fighting the Osages who dominated the prairie-plains region between the Missouri and Arkansas rivers. In the 1820s, the Shawnees and their neighbors worked to build a confederacy, both to wage war against the Osages and to increase their leverage in dealing with the United States.[24]

The far-ranging Shawnees also earned a reputation as

hunters and guides in the West, as did the Delawares, who, like them, moved repeatedly ahead of the advancing frontier. Captain Randolph Marcy, who wrote *The Prairie Traveler* in 1859 as a guidebook for wagon trains crossing the Great Plains, recommended employing Shawnee and Delaware scouts and hunters. He had used them on several occasions and "found them intelligent, brave, reliable, and in every respect well qualified to fill their positions. They are endowed with those keen and wonderful powers in woodcraft which can only be acquired by instinct, practice, and necessity, and which are possessed by no other people that I have heard of, unless it be the khebirs or guides who escort the caravans across the great desert of Sahara." Marcy noted that the Shawnees were closely associated with the Delawares. They were also "familiar with many of the habits and customs of their pale-faced neighbors." Some spoke English, "yet many of their native characteristics cling tenaciously to them."[25]

In Kansas, the Ohio Shawnees rebuilt their lives and their communities. It was not an easy task. They reunited with Shawnees who had migrated from Ohio to Missouri, some more than fifty years before. Most of these earlier emigrants were from the Thawekila and Pekowi divisions. Which groups and individuals would exercise political influence now that the various groups were reunited? Putting the Shawnees back together in one place did not cement the fragmented bands into a single nation, nor did moving them to a western reservation shield them from the pressures that pursued them. Whiskey peddlers; Baptist, Methodist, and Quaker missionaries; and government agents continued to be active among the Shawnees. Shawnees debated over what type of governmental structure they should have, and who should lead them. The Ohio bands, which had more experience dealing with the United States, took the leadership roles, and a new type of Shawnee leader emerged to deal with a new world. Instead of hereditary chiefs leading individual bands and villages, elected leaders working closely with the government and missionaries came to dominate the Shawnee nation that was consolidated on the reservation. George Blue Jacket, grandson of the famous chief, was educated by missionaries and became a Methodist minister as well as Shawnee chief. Joseph Parks, an economically successful and politically connected Shawnee of mixed descent but with no hereditary claim to leadership, mediated relations between the Shawnees and the United States. Many Shawnee people felt distanced from their leaders. One group, the Black Bob band of Chillicothes, consistently opposed the policies and the growing power of the new leadership.[26]

Despite the political conflicts that accompanied the shifts in leadership, the Shawnees did well in Kansas. Henry Harvey said that in 1854 they numbered about nine hundred people—several hundred fewer than had inhabited just their principal town a century before. But they owned about 1.6

million acres of land and had horses, cattle, hogs, sheep, and oxen. They drove farm wagons and even some carriages and buggies. They had plenty of farm implements and grew an "abundance" of corn and oats and some wheat. Many of them lived in good houses, which were "generally very neat; built of hewn logs, with shingled roofs, stone chimneys, and the inside work very well finished off, and mostly done by themselves, as there are a number of very good mechanics among the younger class." The furniture was "useful and respectable furniture" and "kept in good order by the females." Harvey said: "They live in the same manner as the whites do, and live well too."[27] Yet their surface adaptation to American ways obscured a deeper Shawnee conservatism. A Kansas minister said they clung to their old customs and seemed "more reluctant to abandon their ancient rites than any other civilized tribe."[28]

The Shawnees survived the nightmare of removal, started over, and reconstructed their communities, blending American and Shawnee ways. But American demands for Shawnee land soon resumed. "Alas! For this people, who were told that, in case they should sell their lands in Ohio, and remove to this very land, that it should be their home forever," wrote Henry Harvey. Who would have believed that "in less than twenty-five years, the United States should consider this term 'forever' at an end?" In 1854, Kansas was organized into a United States territory and opened to settlement. Settlers flooded into the region and began to claim lands. The 1.6-million-acre Shawnee reservation rapidly dwindled to about two hundred thousand acres in three clusters. Most Shawnees accepted allotments of two hundred acres, although some leaders received substantially larger amounts. The Black Bob band refused to take allotments and held on to communal land across the Missouri line.[29]

But American pressure continued. The Shawnees and their Indian neighbors would have to go. Between 1864 and 1871, the Shawnees from Kansas were removed to Indian Territory. To Henry Harvey, this meant sending them back to "a wild, roving life." Most Shawnees by this time had been "raised up entirely to the pursuits of agriculture," and Harvey warned they had no more idea about how to secure a living as nomadic hunters than did white people.[30] Still, the Shawnees' journeys were not over. When the government began to push for the allotment of Indian lands, the Absentee Shawnees divided over the issue. Almost half the tribe, labeled the "nonprogressives" by the government, refused to accept the allotments. Led by a chief called Big Jim, they moved to the Kickapoo reservation in 1876. Ten years later the government moved them out. In 1900, evidently caught up in some kind of scheme to move the Shawnees to Mexico, Big Jim and some followers moved again, to a Kickapoo reservation at Nacimiento, west of the town of Sabinas in Coahuila. Finding smallpox there, they turned and headed for home, but the

Mexican authorities quarantined them on the bank of the Sabina River. Big Jim and all but two of the group died.[31]

The much-traveled Shawnees had reassembled in Ohio in the second half of the eighteenth century, and in Kansas in the 1830s. In the second half of the nineteenth century they reassembled in Oklahoma, in what was then Indian Territory. The Absentee Shawnees from Texas settled with the Potawatomis. Most of the Shawnees from Kansas moved to the Cherokee reservation in 1869, were incorporated with the Cherokee Nation three years later, and became known as the Cherokee Shawnees or Loyal Shawnees (testimony to their pro-Union sentiments during the Civil War). Those Shawnees who had moved west with Senecas from Lewistown in 1832 separated from them in 1867 and became known as the Eastern Shawnees. In 2000, the Cherokee Shawnees separated from the Cherokee Nation and received federal recognition as a distinct Indian tribe.[32]

Time and again in the war for America, the Shawnees were forced to surrender their lands and move on. But there are things they have never surrendered. The official website of the Absentee Shawnee in Oklahoma contains a simple but clear statement:

> The Absentee Shawnee Tribe possesses all the inherent powers of sovereignty held prior to the Constitution of the United States. The inherent right of

self-government precedes the United States Constitution, and the governing body of the Absentee Shawnee has never relinquished any part of this sovereign right. Among the powers of self-government upheld by the actions of the Absentee Shawnee, are the power to adopt and operate a form of government of their choosing, to define the conditions of tribal membership, to regulate domestic relations of members, to levy taxes, to regulate property within the jurisdiction of the Tribe, to control the conduct of membership by legislation and to administer justice.[33]

The war for America is over, but throughout America, Native people and Native ways survive. So do Native nations—more than 560 of them in the lower forty-eight states and Alaska.

AFTERWORD

BATTLES OVER HISTORY—dry, old history—and whose history gets to be told can become heated and emotional because the ways we behaved then say so much about the kind of people, society, or nation we have become. Nations, like people, find important elements of identity in the past; they draw moral lessons from it, and they point to it as a source of guiding values. Individuals, societies, and nations all tell their own stories about the past, and they remember, interpret, and imagine it in their own ways. When different historical experiences result from shared events, history becomes a contested ground where alternative versions of the past vie for supremacy, and where some people's voices struggle just to be heard. As they did on the Ohio River in the late eighteenth century, battle lines harden because the contest is not just about history, as it was then not just about land. It is also about whose vision of America should prevail.

Americans conquered the continent, occupied the land, and transformed the landscape, beyond all recognition in many places. But contests continue. Some Indian groups continue to fight for the land, or at least some of it, although their battles are now waged in courtrooms. And people disagree, sometimes vehemently, about what happened in the past and about which histories should be told. The Shawnees' homelands figured prominently in the growth and development of the United States, and the events that occurred there, and the meanings attached to those events, matter to the nation's sense of itself.

Writing at the end of the nineteenth century, historian Frederick Jackson Turner argued that the frontier and the process of westward expansion shaped the American nation and the American character.[1] America's pioneer heritage continues to be credited with generating many of America's core values, and its stories form a central part of the nation's history. But the stories and the values they carry emerged over time. Elizabeth Perkins, in her study of historical experience and memory in the Ohio Valley, notes that as the original combatants died off, new generations of historians and writers "shaped their accounts along increasingly racist and nationalistic lines." The settlers' own stories were "often tinged with ambivalence or regret," but "later conquest narratives breathed moral certainty." Pioneers were heroes, Indians inhuman. A long and bloody war that had sometimes hung in the balance now became "the inevitable triumph of a superior race."[2] God-fearing pioneers carving out new lives, bringing civilization to a wilderness, and extending the blessings of liberty, democracy, and equality provide cherished images of nation-building. But what if our pioneer forefathers also butchered Indian families, stole Indian lands, broke treaties, desecrated the environment, and destroyed societies that were truly free and egalitarian?

Some people refuse to contemplate such things, and dismiss such suggestions as attempts to rewrite history with some kind of anti-American agenda. Many historians, however, insist that it is essential to paint as full a picture as possible of the past and to consider multiple historical experiences; otherwise we perpetuate a mythic past that offers little guidance for the real world. History and humans, even in America, have their dark sides. Indians had no monopoly on cruelty, vengefulness, and treachery, and no one has a monopoly on courage and love of freedom.

Many Indian people insist not only that their stories should be told, but that they, not white historians, should do the telling. Indian voices have been silenced for too long, they say. Enduring colonial structures and attitudes continue to constrain them, and non-Indian historians at their best can only get part of the story right.

Others—then as now—saw both visions of America, and saw value in both. In 1882, Thomas Wildcat Alford returned home after three years at Hampton Institute, brim full of information and ideas to help his people. His homecoming was a disappointment. Noticing the change in his dress, speech, manner, and behavior, "My people received me coldly and with suspicion." They suspected that along with the white man's education he had taken on the white man's religion and conduct. It was an experience shared by thousands of Indian students returning from boarding schools and colleges in the East. Alford became a schoolteacher on the reservation. He also translated the Gospels into Shawnee, thereby promoting Christianity among his people while at the same time helping to preserve their language. He stood at the intersection of two cultures and two ways of life, and could comment on both from personal experience. Even as he worked to bring Shawnee children more fully into American culture, he knew the values and worth of Shawnee culture; even as he looked to the future, he understood the importance of the past, and of the struggle the Shawnees had waged. "My people were among those who once owned this vast country," he wrote; "they were strong and brave and virtuous, according to their knowledge. If they have failed to live up to the standards of the white race, they at least have fought for their own convictions. Who can say that in future generations they will not contribute something of untold value to the life of our nation?"[3]

Perhaps they already had done so. In defending a world that had its own order and values, its own civilization, the Shawnees fought for a different vision of America. In many ways, it is a fight that continues as Americans struggle to accommodate different visions of America, and of the world.

ACKNOWLEDGMENTS

I AM GRATEFUL to executive editor Carolyn Carlson for the invitation to do this series, and to her and associate editor Ellen Garrison for suggestions that significantly improved the book. I am indebted to R. David Edmunds and John P. Bowes for reading the manuscript, and to Jason Hartwig for assistance in obtaining copies of documents. My debts to the many fine scholars who have researched and written on the history of the Shawnees and the struggle for America's heartland will be evident in the notes.

NOTES

INTRODUCTION

1. Reverend David Jones, *A Journal of Two Visits made to some Nations of Indians on the West Side of the Ohio River, in the Years 1772 and 1773* (Burlington, VT: Isaac Collins printer, 1774), 37 (Piqua), 38–39 (Hardman), 46–48 (encounter with Yellow Hawk).

2. Herman Wellenreuther and Carola Wessel, eds., *The Moravian Mission Diaries of David Zeisberger, 1772–1781* (University Park: Pennsylvania State University Press, 2005), 129–30.

3. Wellenreuther and Wessel, eds., *The Moravian Mission Diaries of David Zeisberger,* 165–66, 172.

4. Lillian M. Hawes, ed., "The Papers of Lachlan McIntosh, 1774–1779," *Collections of the Georgia Historical Society* 12 (1957), 160.

5. Correspondence and Papers of Sir Frederick Haldimand, British Museum, Additional Mss. 21782: 302 (hereafter, Haldimand Papers).

6. Stephen Aron, *How the West Was Lost: The Transformation of*

Kentucky from Daniel Boone to Henry Clay (Baltimore: Johns Hopkins University Press, 1996), 197.

7. Elizabeth A. Perkins, *Border Life: Experience and Memory in the Revolutionary Ohio Valley* (Chapel Hill: University of North Carolina Press, 1998), 69.

8. Matilda Edgar, ed., *Ten Years of Upper Canada in Peace and War, 1805–1815, Being the Ridout letters . . . Also An Appendix of the Captivity among the Shawanese Indians, in 1788 of Thos. Ridout* (Toronto: William Briggs, 1890), 356.

9. Clara Sue Kidwell and Alan Velie, "Land and Identity," in their *Native American Studies* (Lincoln: University of Nebraska Press, 2005), ch. 2.

10. Nancy Shoemaker, *A Strange Likeness: Becoming Red and White in Eighteenth Century North America* (New York: Oxford University Press, 2004), 29.

11. Peter Nabokov, *Where the Lightning Strikes: The Lives of American Indian Sacred Places* (New York: Viking/Penguin, 2006), xv.

12. Charles Callender, "Shawnee," in Bruce G. Trigger, ed., *Handbook of North American Indians. 15: Northeast* (Washington, D.C.: Smithsonian Institution, 1978), 624.

13. Larry L. Nelson, ed., *A History of Jonathan Alder: His Captivity and Life with the Indians* (Akron: University of Akron Press, 2003), 120.

14. Richard Butler's word list, reproduced in Dark Rain Thom, *Kohkumthena's Grandchildren: The Shawnee* (Indianapolis: Guild Press of Indiana, 1994), 273; Haldimand Papers 21845: 483, quoted in John Sugden, *Blue Jacket: Warrior of the Shawnees* (Lincoln: University of Nebraska Press, 2000), 46.

15. Vernon Kinietz and Erminie W. Voegelin, eds., *Shawnese Traditions: C. C. Trowbridge's Account* (Ann Arbor: University of Michigan, 1939), 48; Philip Levy, *Fellow Travelers: Indians and Europeans Contesting the Early American Trail* (University Press

of Florida, forthcoming), ch. 4, contrasts Indian and European reactions to rattlesnakes.

16. Leonard W. Labaree, ed., *The Papers of Benjamin Franklin*, 35 vols. (New Haven: Yale University Press, 1959–99), 4: 481–83; Warren Barton Blake, ed., *Letters from an American Farmer*, by Hector St. John de Crèvecoeur (London: J. M. Dent, 1962), 214–16.

17. Colin G. Calloway, *New Worlds for All: Indians, Europeans, and the Remaking of Early America* (Baltimore: Johns Hopkins University Press, 1997); Perkins, *Border Life*; *The Diary of David McClure 1748–1820* (1899; reprinted Waterville, Ohio: Rettig's Frontier Ohio, 1996), 93; Sugden, *Blue Jacket*.

18. Virginia DeJohn Anderson, *Creatures of Empire: How Domestic Animals Transformed Early America* (New York: Oxford University Press, 2004), discusses the impact of animals in New England and the Chesapeake.

19. Shoemaker, *A Strange Likeness*.

20. James Sullivan, et al., eds., *The Papers of Sir William Johnson*, 15 vols. (Albany: State University of New York Press, 1921–65) 11: 394.

21. See, for example, Thomas Wildcat Alford, *Civilization and the Story of the Absentee Shawnees* (Norman: University of Oklahoma Press, 1936), and Dark Rain Thom, *Kohkumthena's Grandchildren*.

CHAPTER I

1. Wilbur R. Jacobs, ed., *The Appalachian Indian Frontier: The Edmund Atkin Report and Plan of 1755* (Lincoln: University of Nebraska Press, 1967), 65.

2. Blue Jacket explained the Shawnees' relationships with other tribes at the Treaty of Greenville in 1795; *The New American State Papers: Indian Affairs*, Vol. 4 (Wilmington, DE: Scholarly Resources, Inc., 1972), 162.

3. Thomas Wildcat Alford, *Civilization and the Story of the Absentee Shawnees* (Norman: University of Oklahoma Press, 1936), 44; Vernon Kinietz and Erminie W. Voegelin, eds., *Shawnese Traditions: C. C. Trowbridge's Account* (Ann Arbor: University of Michigan, 1939), 16–17.

4. Kinietz and Voegelin, eds., *Shawnese Traditions: C. C. Trowbridge's Account*, 37, 55–56, 61.

5. Reuben G. Thwaites, ed., *The Jesuit Relations and Allied Documents,* 73 vols. (Cleveland: Burrows Bros, 1896–1901), 59: 144–45; James H. Howard, *Shawnee!: The Ceremonialism of a Native American Tribe and Its Cultural Background* (Athens, OH: Ohio University Press, 1981), 5.

6. The tribe rarely migrated as a whole: usually one or two divisions, or small bands drawn from the divisions, would move. On Shawnee migrations, see Jerry E. Clark, *The Shawnee* (Lexington: University Press of Kentucky, 1993), ch. 2; Howard, *Shawnee*, 7–8.

7. Henry Harvey, *History of the Shawnee Indians, from the Year 1681 to 1854* (Cincinnati: Ephraim Morgan and Sons, 1855), 84.

8. Donald H. Kent, ed., *Pennsylvania and Delaware Treaties, 1629–1737*, in Alden T. Vaughan, gen. ed., *Early American Indian Documents: Treaties and Laws, 1607–1789*, 20 vols. (Fredericksburg and Bethesda, MD: University Publications of America, 1979–2004), Vol. 1: 336, 338–39, 363–67, quotation at 366.

9. Randolph C. Downes, *Council Fires on the Upper Ohio: A Narrative of Indian Affairs in the Upper Ohio Valley until 1795* (Pittsburgh: University of Pittsburgh Press, 1940), ch. 2; Donald H. Kent, ed., *Pennsylvania Treaties, 1737–1756*, in Vaughan, gen. ed., *Early American Indian Documents.* Vol. 2: 1–2, 5–6, 10–17, 181–82, 263, 443.

10. Lois Mulkearn, ed., *George Mercer Papers Relating to the Ohio Company of Virginia* (Pittsburgh: University of Pittsburgh Press, 1954), 16.

11. Michael N. McConnell, *A Country Between: The Upper Ohio Valley and Its Peoples, 1724–1774* (Lincoln: University of Nebraska Press, 1992), chs. 1–2.

12. Alford, *Civilization and the Story of the Absentee Shawnees*, 15–17.

13. Edward Denning Andrews, "The Shaker Mission to the Shawnee Indians," *Winterthur Portfolio* 7 (1972), 126.

14. Kinietz and Voegelin, eds., *Shawnese Traditions: C. C. Trowbridge's Account*, 12–13.

15. Harvey, *History of the Shawnee Indians*, 51–52.

16. Reverend David Jones, *A Journal of Two Visits made to some Nations of Indians on the West Side of the River Ohio, in the Years 1772 and 1773* (Burlington, VT: Isaac Collins, printer, 1774), 54.

17. Gregory Evans Dowd, *A Spirited Resistance: The North American Indian Struggle for Unity, 1745–1815* (Baltimore: Johns Hopkins University Press, 1992), 40–45.

18. Charles A. Stuart, ed., *Memoir of Indian Wars and Other Occurrences, By the late Colonel Stuart of Greenbrier* (New York: Arno Press, Inc., 1971), 49.

19. Carl F. Klinck and James J. Talman, eds., *The Journal of Major John Norton 1816* (Toronto: The Champlain Society, 1970), 188–89; Jones, *A Journal of Two Visits*, 52–53.

20. Klinck and Talman, eds., *The Journal of Major John Norton 1816*, 189.

21. Jones, *A Journal of Two Visits*, 62–63. A young Englishman provided a similar description of Shawnee men a year later: *The Journal of Nicholas Cresswell*, 1774–1777 (New York: Dial, 1924), 50.

22. Milo M. Quaife, ed., *The Indian Captivity of O. M. Spencer* (New York: Citadel Press, 1968), 87–88.

23. Clark, *The Shawnee*, end map.

CHAPTER 2

1. Michael N. McConnell, *A Country Between: The Upper Ohio Valley and Its Peoples, 1724–1774* (Lincoln: University of Nebraska Press, 1992).

2. Donald H. Kent., ed., *Pennsylvania Treaties, 1737–1756,* in Alden T. Vaughan, gen. ed., *Early American Indian Documents: Treaties and Laws, 1607–1789* (Fredericksburg and Bethesda, MD: University Publications of America, 1979–2004), Vol. 2: 77–110; James H. Merrell, ed., *The Lancaster Treaty of 1744* (Boston: Bedford/St. Martins, 2007).

3. Lois Mulkearn, ed., *George Mercer Papers Relating to the Ohio Company of Virginia* (Pittsburgh: University of Pittsburgh Press, 1954), 9–10, 39.

4. Charles Morse Stotz, *Outposts of the War for Empire: The French and English in Western Pennsylvania* (Pittsburgh: Historical Society of Western Pennsylvania/University of Pittsburgh Press, 1985), 4. Stotz identifies the old chief, Kakowatchiky, as Seneca, but McConnell, *A Country Between*, 28–29, 62, shows him to have been Shawnee.

5. Randolph C. Downes, *Council Fires on the Upper Ohio* (Pittsburgh: University of Pittsburgh Press, 1940), 57–58; Kent, ed., *Pennsylvania Treaties, 1737–1756,* 263.

6. "Journal of James Kenny," *Pennsylvania Magazine of History and Biography,* 37 (1913), 183.

7. Ian Steele, "Shawnee Origins of Their Seven Years' War," *Ethnohistory* 53 (2006), 657–87. For the full story of the war in that area, see Matthew C. Ward, *Breaking the Backcountry: The Seven Years' War in Virginia and Pennsylvania, 1754–1765* (Pittsburgh: University of Pittsburgh Press, 2003).

8. Ian K. Steele, "The Shawnees and the English: Captives and War, 1753–1756," in Daniel P. Barr, ed., *The Boundaries Between Us: Natives and Newcomers along the Frontiers of the Old North-*

west Territory, 1750–1850 (Kent, OH: Kent State University Press, 2006), 1–24; Kent, ed., *Pennsylvania Treaties, 1737–1756*, 465.

9. Larry L. Nelson, ed., *A History of Jonathan Alder: His Captivity and Life with the Indians* (Akron: University of Akron Press, 2003), 45; Milo M. Quaife, ed., "Henry Hay's Journal from Detroit to the Miami River," *Proceedings of the State Historical Society of Wisconsin*, 62 (1915), 208–61; McMullen at 248–49.

10. James Sullivan et al., eds., *The Papers of Sir William Johnson*, 15 vols. (Albany: State University of New York Press, 1921–65) 9: 591.

11. "Conference at Fort Pitt," April 7–12, 1760, Alison Duncan Hirsch, ed., *Pennsylvania Treaties, 1756–1775*, in Vaughan, gen. ed., *Early American Indian Documents*, Vol. 3: 544–45.

12. Sir Jeffery, First Baron Amherst, Official Papers and Correspondence, 1740–83, 202 reels (London: World Microfilm Publications, 1979; hereafter Amherst Papers), reel 32: 154; "Journal of James Kenny," *Pennsylvania Magazine of History and Biography*, 37 (1913), 156–57; Bouquet to Amherst, May 24, 1762, Amherst Papers, reel 32: 154.

13. "Journal of Alexander McKee," in Sullivan et al., eds., *The Papers of Sir William Johnson*, 10: 578; "Journal of James Kenny," 169, 172.

14. "Journal of Alexander McKee," 576–80; Amherst Papers, reel 30: 216–17 (quotes).

15. Larry L. Nelson, *A Man of Distinction Among Them: Alexander McKee and the Ohio Country Frontier, 1754–1799* (Kent, OH: Kent State University Press, 1999), 39.

16. Gregory Evans Dowd, *A Spirited Resistance: The North American Indian Struggle for Unity, 1745–1815* (Baltimore: Johns Hopkins University Press, 1992), 36–40.

17. Armand Francis Lucier, comp., *Pontiac's Conspiracy and Other Indian Affairs: Notices Abstracted from Colonial Newspapers,*

1763–1765 (Bowie, MD: Heritage Books, 2000), 143; *Papers of Henry Bouquet* 6: 261–62; also quoted in Francis Parkman, *The Conspiracy of Pontiac*, 2 vols. (New York: E. P. Dutton and Co., 1908) 2: 15.

18. The smallpox blankets were actually distributed before Amherst urged the use of germ warfare. Elizabeth A. Fenn, "Biological Warfare in Eighteenth-Century North America: Beyond Jeffery Amherst," *Journal of American History*, 86 (2000), 1552–80, weighs the evidence against Amherst, traces the long-standing debate about whether he ordered germ warfare, and considers the broader context for the application of such tactics.

19. "Gladwin Manuscripts," *Collections of the Michigan Pioneer and Historical Society,* 27 (1897), 671–72.

20. Clarence Edwin Carter, ed., *The Correspondence of General Thomas Gage*, 2 vols. (New Haven: Yale University Press, 1933) 1: 37–40 (quote at 39).

21. William Smith, *An Historical Account of the Expedition against the Ohio Indians in the year 1764* (Philadelphia, 1766), 17–21; "Bouquet Papers," *Collections of the Michigan Pioneer and Historical Society*, 19 (1892), 279–82.

22. Smith, *An Historical Account of the Expedition against the Ohio Indians*, 25–37.

23. The talks at Fort Pitt are in Public Record Office, Colonial Office Records, C.O.5/66: 93–98.

24. Edmund B. O'Callaghan, ed., *Documents Relating to the Colonial History of the State of New York,* 15 vols. (Albany: Weed, Parsons, 1853–1887) 7: 750–55.

25. "Croghan's Journal, 1765," in Reuben G. Thwaites, ed., *Early Western Journals, 1748–1765* (Lewisburg, PA: Wennawoods Publishing, 1998), 139.

26. National Archives of Scotland, "Journal of a Detachment of the 42nd Regiment from Fort Pitt down the Ohio to the Country of the Illenoise," GD 298/196: 59–63. This chief has been

identified as Cornstalk but the evidence and location suggest Kaské.

CHAPTER 3

1. Minutes of a Conference held at Fort Pitt, April and May 1768, in *Iroquois Indians: A Documentary History*, 50 microfilm reels (Woodbridge, CT: 1984), quoted in Gregory Evans Dowd, *War Under Heaven: Pontiac, the Indian Nations, and the British Empire* (Baltimore: Johns Hopkins University Press, 2002), 216.

2. Quoted in Fred Anderson, *Crucible of War: The Seven Years' War and the Fate of Empire in British North America, 1754–1766* (New York: Alfred Knopf, 2000), 740.

3. Peter Marshall, "Sir William Johnson and the Treaty of Fort Stanwix, 1768," *Journal of American Studies*, 1 (1967), 149–79. The proceedings and deed of the Treaty of Fort Stanwix are in Edmund B. O'Callaghan, ed., *Documents Relating to the Colonial History of the State of New York*, 15 vols. (Albany: Weed, Parsons, 1853–1887) 8: 111–34.

4. Wilbur R. Jacobs, *Dispossessing the American Indian* (New York: Scribners, 1972), 100.

5. James Sullivan, et al., eds., *The Papers of Sir William Johnson*, 15 vols. (Albany: University of the State of New York, 1921–1965), 7: 182; Larry L. Nelson, *A Man of Distinction Among Them: Alexander McKee and the Ohio Country Frontier, 1754–1799* (Kent, OH: Kent State University Press, 1999).

6. Sullivan, et al., eds., *The Papers of Sir William Johnson*, 7: 184; K. G. Davies, ed., *Documents of the American Revolution 1770–1783* (Colonial Office Series), 20 vols. (Shannon: Irish University Press, 1972), 2: 22.

7. Sullivan, et al., eds., *The Papers of Sir William Johnson*, 7: 184, 406–8; Davies, ed., *Documents of the American Revolution*, 1: 159, 315; 2: 22, 24, 28, 87, 105, 204, 253–54, 261–62.

8. Public Record Office, London, Colonial Office Records, C.O.5/71: 41; Davies, ed., *Documents of the American Revolution*, 2: 203–4.

9. Davies, ed., *Documents of the American Revolution*, 3: 43.

10. Colonial Office Records, C.O.5/72: 311.

11. Stephen Aron, *How the West Was Lost: The Transformation of Kentucky from Daniel Boone to Henry Clay* (Baltimore: Johns Hopkins University Press, 1996), 18–19; John Mack Faragher, *Daniel Boone, The Life and Legend of an American Pioneer* (New York: Henry Holt, 1992), 76–81.

12. Faragher, *Daniel Boone*, 89–97; Sullivan, et al., eds., *The Papers of Sir William Johnson*, 12: 1038–39.

13. Pioneer quoted in Faragher, *Daniel Boone*, 123; Aron, *How the West Was Lost*, ch. 1; idem., "Pigs and Hunters: 'Rights in the Woods' on the Trans-Appalachian Frontier," in Andrew R. L. Clayton and Frederick J. Teute, eds., *Contact Points: American Frontiers from the Mohawk Valley to the Mississippi, 1750–1830* (Chapel Hill: University of North Carolina Press, 1998), 175–204.

14. "Conference with Kayaghshota," in Sullivan, et al., eds., *The Papers of Sir William Johnson*, 12: 1044–61 (quotes at 1045, 1053); Colonial Office Records, C.O.5/74: 173; C.O.5/75: 142.

15. Reuben Gold Thwaites and Louise Phelps Kellogg, eds., *Documentary History of Dunmore's War, 1774* (Madison: Wisconsin Historical Society, 1905), provides a compilation of materials relating to the war from the Lyman C. Draper Manuscripts in the Wisconsin State Historical Society.

16. McKee, "Journal of Negotiations with Indians at Pittsburgh," 10.

17. *Pennsylvania Archives*, first series, 4: 570.

18. C.O.5/75: 228, 241, 254; Jack M. Sosin, "The British Indian Department and Dunmore's War," *Virginia Magazine of History and Biography*, 74 (1966), 34–50.

19. Herman Wellenreuther and Carola Wessel, eds., *The Moravian Mission Diaries of David Zeisberger, 1772–1781* (University Park: Pennsylvania State University Press, 2005), 216.

20. Thwaites and Kellogg, eds., *Documentary History of Dunmore's War*, 91–92.

21. Thwaites and Kellogg, eds., *Documentary History of Dunmore's War*, 114–15.

22. Thwaites and Kellogg, eds., *Documentary History of Dunmore's War*, 151–56.

23. Charles A. Stuart, ed., *Memoir of Indian Wars, and Other Occurrences, by the Late Colonel Stuart, of Greenbrier* (New York: The New York Times and Arno Press reprint, 1971), 46–48; Thwaites and Kellogg, eds., *Documentary History of Dunmore's War*, 256, 259, 265, 275, 343, 346 (scalps), and 261–66 (Christian's account); Carl F. Klinck and James J. Talman, eds., *The Journal of Major John Norton, 1816* (Toronto: The Champlain Society, 1970), 16–17, 52–53.

24. Lyman C. Draper Manuscripts, Wisconsin Historical Society, 9BB: 63, 8ZZ: 71; Thwaites and Kellogg, eds., *Documentary History of Dunmore's War*, 422n.

25. Stuart, *Memoir of Indian Wars, and Other Occurrences*, 49.

26. Stuart, *Memoir of Indian Wars, and Other Occurrences*, 62.

27. Reginald Horsman, *Matthew Elliott, British Indian Agent* (Detroit: Wayne State University Press, 1964), 5–6.

28. *The Journal of Nicholas Cresswell, 1774–1777* (New York: Dial, 1924), 50.

29. Thomas Wildcat Alford, *Civilization and the Story of the Absentee Shawnees* (Norman: University of Oklahoma Press, 1936), 200–201.

30. Robert L. Scribner, et al., eds. *Revolutionary Virginia, The Road to Independence: A Documentary Record*, 7 vols. (Charlottesville: University Press of Virginia, 1973–83), 7: 770.

31. Shawnee experiences in the war are covered in Colin G. Callo-way, *The American Revolution in Indian Country* (Cambridge: Cambridge University Press, 1995), ch. 5, which focuses on the Mekoche or Maquachake division and also provides fuller documentation.

32. Stuart's account is in C.O.5/77: 169, and printed in William L. Saunders and Walter Clark, eds., *The Colonial and State Records of North Carolina*, 30 vols. (Raleigh: Dept. of State, 1886–90), 10: 660–61; 763–85; and Davies, ed., *Documents of the American Revolution*, 12: 191–208, esp. 202–3.

33. Faragher, *Daniel Boone*, 131–40; Jemima quoted at 140.

34. Horsman, *Matthew Elliott*, 11–12.

35. The negotiations of Cornstalk and other Shawnee chiefs with Morgan, and Cornstalk's speech to Congress, November 7, 1776, are in "Letter Book of George Morgan 1776," Pennsylvania Historical Commission, Harrisburg, PA.

36. Carnegie Library of Pittsburgh, Colonel George Morgan Letterbooks, 3 vols., 1775–79, Vol. 1: 57.

37. Wellenreuther and Wessel, eds., *The Moravian Mission Diaries of David Zeisberger*, 358.

38. Reuben G. Thwaites and Louise P. Kellogg, eds., *The Revolution on the Upper Ohio, 1775–1777* (Madison: Wisconsin State Historical Society, 1908), 14–15; Draper Mss., Wisconsin State Historical Society, 2YY92; Saunders and Clark, eds., *Colonial and State Records of North Carolina*, 10: 386; George Morgan Letterbooks, 1: 47–48, 57, 85.

39. Draper Mss. 1U68; National Archives Microfilm, *Papers of the Continental Congress*, reel 180, item 163: 278; Reuben G. Thwaites and Louise P. Kellogg, eds., *Frontier Defense on the Upper Ohio, 1777–1778* (Madison: Wisconsin Historical Society, 1912), 20, 25.

40. On Cornstalk's murder, see Stuart, ed., *Memoir of Indian Wars*, 58–62; Draper Mss. 3D164-73, 2YY91-94; Thwaites and Kel-

logg, eds., *Frontier Defense on the Upper Ohio,* 126–27, 149, 157–63, 175–77, 188–89, 205–9, 258–61.

41. Papers of the Continental Congress, reel 37, item 30: 371–73; reel 69, item 56: 169–70. Dark Rain and James Alexander Thom, *Warrior Woman: A Novel Based on the Life of Nonhelema, Shawnee Woman Chief* (New York: Ballantine Books, 2003), is a fictional account based on close reading of the historical record.

42. Thwaites and Kellogg, eds., *Frontier Defense,* 166, 242; Louise P. Kellogg, ed., *Frontier Advance on the Upper Ohio 1778–1779* (Madison: Wisconsin Historical Society, 1916), 91, 110, 143, 193, 234, 245; George Morgan Letterbooks, 3: 27, 54, 56, 96.

CHAPTER 4

1. Gregory Evans Dowd, *A Spirited Resistance: The North American Indian Struggle for Unity, 1745–1815* (Baltimore: Johns Hopkins University Press, 1992), ch. 3.

2. John Mack Faragher, *Daniel Boone: The Life and Legend of an American Pioneer* (New York: Henry Holt, 1992), 154–202.

3. Thomas Wildcat Alford, *Civilization and the Story of the Absentee Shawnees* (Norman: University of Oklahoma Press, 1936), 200–202.

4. Louise P. Kellogg, ed., *Frontier Advance on the Upper Ohio, 1778–1779* (Madison: Wisconsin State Historical Society, 1916), 279–80, 349.

5. British Museum, Haldimand Papers, 21782: 246.

6. Julian P. Boyd, ed., *The Papers of Thomas Jefferson,* 32 vols. to date (Princeton University Press, 1950–) 3: 259, 276.

7. Haldimand Papers, 21781: 74.

8. Accounts of the expedition are compiled in J. Martin West, ed., *Clark's Shawnee Campaign of 1780: Contemporary Accounts* (Springfield, OH: The Clark County Historical Society, 1975).

9. *Collections of the Michigan Pioneer Historical Society*, 10: 462–65.

10. Zeisberger quoted in Dowd, *Spirited Resistance*, 88.

11. Faragher, *Daniel Boone*, 216–25.

12. "Journal of Daniel Boone," *Ohio Archaeological and Historical Publications*, 13 (1904), 276; Draper Mss. 1AA, 276–77.

13. Colin G. Calloway, *Crown and Calumet: British-Indian Relations, 1783–1815* (Norman: University of Oklahoma Press, 1987), 3–23; Public Record Office, Colonial Office Records, C.O.42/44: 264–65; Haldimand Papers, 21763: 207–09.

14. Haldimand Papers, 21779: 117.

15. *Collections of the Michigan Pioneer Historical Society*, 20: 176.

16. Quoted in Colin G. Calloway, *The American Revolution in Indian Country* (Cambridge: Cambridge University Press, 1995), vi, 281.

17. Colin G. Calloway, ed., *Revolution and Confederation*, in Alden T. Vaughan, gen. ed., *Early American Indian Documents: Treaties and Laws, 1607–1789*, 20 vols. (Bethesda, MD: University Publications of America, 1979–2004), Vol. 18: 284, 313–27.

18. British Museum, Miscellaneous American Papers, Additional Mss., 24,322: 98–99, 112–13.

19. C.O.42/48: 211.

20. The negotiations at Fort Finney are described in *The Military Journal of Major Ebenezer Denny* (Philadelphia: J.B. Lippincot & Co., 1859), 63 ff., and the "Journal of General Richard Butler at the Treaty of Fort Finney," in Neville B. Craig, ed., *The Olden Time*, 2 vols. (Pittsburgh, 1848), 2: 510–31. Excerpts from Butler's journal and the treaty itself are reprinted in Calloway, ed., *Revolution and Confederation*, 340–51. The treaty is also in Charles J. Kappler, comp., *Indian Affairs: Laws and Treaties*, 2 vols. (Washington, DC: Government Printing Office, 1904) 2: 16–18.

21. Quoted in Calloway, *American Revolution in Indian Country*, 48.

22. Calloway, ed., *Revolution and Confederation*, 158.

23. Craig, ed., *The Olden Time*, 2: 515.

24. National Archives Microfilm, Papers of the Continental Congress, reel 69, item 56: 378.

25. Papers of the Continental Congress, reel 164, item 150, Vol. 1: 265, 431–33.

26. "Logan's Campaign—1786," *Ohio Archaeological and Historical Publications*, 22 (1913), 520–21; *The Military Journal of Major Ebenezer Denny*, 94.

CHAPTER 5

1. Carl F. Klinck and James J. Talman, eds., *The Journal of Major John Norton 1816* (Toronto: The Champlain Society, 1970), 176.

2. This chapter relies heavily on John Sugden's excellent biography, *Blue Jacket: Warrior of the Shawnees* (Lincoln: University of Nebraska Press, 2000).

3. Sugden, *Blue Jacket*, 54; Matilda Edgar, ed., *Ten Years of Upper Canada in Peace and War, 1805–1815, Being the Ridout letters . . . Also An Appendix of the Captivity among the Shawanese Indians, in 1788 of Thos. Ridout* (Toronto: William Briggs, 1890), 366.

4. Milo M. Quaife, ed., *The Indian Captivity of O. M. Spencer* (New York: Citadel Press, 1968), 89–92.

5. On the movement of Indian towns see Helen H. Tanner and Erminie Wheeler Voegelin, *Indians of Ohio and Indiana Prior to 1795*, 2 vols. (New York: Garland Press, 1975), esp. 2: 532–36, 553 ff., and Helen H. Tanner, *Atlas of Great Lakes Indian History* (Norman: University of Oklahoma Press, 1987), 79–91. "General Harmar's daily log," *Ohio Archaeological and Historical Quarterly*, 20: 94.

6. Charles J. Kappler, comp., *Indian Affairs: Laws and Treaties*, 2 vols. (Washington, DC: Government Printing Office, 1904), 2: 18–23.

7. "General Harmar's Expedition," *Ohio Archaeological and Historical Publications*, 20 (1911), 74–108; *The Military Journal of Major Ebenezer Denny* (Philadelphia: J.B. Lippincott & Co., 1859), 146–47; Public Record Office, Colonial Office Records, C.O.42/73: 37.

8. C.O.42/73: 39–40.

9. Colin G. Calloway, *Crown and Calumet: British-Indian Relations, 1783–1815* (Norman: University of Oklahoma Press, 1987).

10. *Collections of the Michigan Pioneer Historical Society*, 12: 305.

11. C.O.42/89: 35.

12. Klinck and Talman, eds., *Journal of Major John Norton*, 178; Quaife, ed., *Indian Captivity of O. M. Spencer*, 28.

13. Helen Hornbeck Tanner, "The Glaize in 1792: A Composite Indian Community," *Ethnohistory*, 25 (Winter 1978), 15–39.

14. Clarence E. Carter, ed., *The Territorial Papers of the United States*, 28 vols. (Washington, DC: Government Printing Office, 1934–1975), 2: 361.

15. "Indian Council at the Glaize, 1792," in E. A. Cruikshank, ed., *The Correspondence of Lieut. Governor John Graves Simcoe, with Allied Documents Relating to His Administration of the Government of Upper Canada*, 5 vols. (Toronto: Ontario Historical Society, 1923–31), 1: 218–29; B. H. Coates, ed., "A Narrative of an Embassy to the Western Indians from the Original Manuscript of Hendrick Aupaumut," *Memoirs of the Historical Society of Pennsylvania*, 2 (1827), pt. 1: 118.

16. Klinck and Talman, eds., *Journal of Major John Norton*, 180.

17. *American State Papers. Class II. Indian Affairs*, 2 vols. (Washington, DC: Gales and Seaton, 1834), 1: 288.

18. Lawrence Kinnaird, ed., *Spain in the Mississippi Valley, 1765–1794: Translations of Materials from the Spanish Archives in the Bancroft Library*, Annual Report of the American Historical Association for 1945, part 3: xxx, 25, 306; Henry Harvey, *History*

of the Shawnee Indians (Cincinnati: Ephraim Morgan and Sons, 1855), 98.

19. Cruikshank, ed., *Simcoe Correspondence*, 1: 355.

20. Cruikshank, ed., *Simcoe Correspondence*, 2: 1–35, contains details of the talks that spring and summer. American accounts are in General Benjamin Lincoln, "Journal of a Treaty held in 1793, with the Indian Tribes northwest of the Ohio by Commissioners of the United States," *Collections of the Massachusetts Historical Society*, 3rd series, 5 (1836), 109–76, and *The New American State Papers: Indian Affairs*, Vol. 4 (Wilmington, DE: Scholarly Resources, Inc., 1972), 120–45.

21. Reginald Horsman, "The British Indian Department and the Abortive Treaty of Lower Sandusky, 1793," *Ohio Historical Quarterly*, 70 (1961), 189–213.

22. *New American State Papers, Indian Affairs*, Vol. 4: 144.

23. The Indian message to the commissioners and the commissioners' response are in Cruikshank, ed., *Simcoe Correspondence*, 2: 17–24, and in *New American State Papers: Indian Affairs*, Vol. 4: 139–41.

24. C.O.42/98: 104–5; Cruikshank, ed., *Simcoe Correspondence*, 2: 149–50.

25. Dresden W. Howard, "The Battle of Fallen Timbers as Told by Chief Kin-Jo-I-No," *Northwest Ohio Quarterly*, 20 (1948), 39.

26. Larry L. Nelson, ed., *A History of Jonathan Alder: His Captivity and Life with the Indians* (Akron: University of Akron Press, 2003), 109.

27. Howard, "The Battle of Fallen Timbers as Told by Chief Kin-Jo-I-No," 47.

28. Cruikshank, ed., *Simcoe Correspondence*, 3: 29.

29. Cruikshank, ed., *Simcoe Correspondence*, 3: 8.

30. Klinck and Talman, eds., *Journal of Major John Norton*, 186.

31. Klinck and Talman, eds., *Journal of Major John Norton*, 187.

32. Sugden, *Blue Jacket*, 192–93, 208; Shawnee complaints against Blue Jacket in Cruikshank, ed., *Simcoe Correspondence*, 3: 288; McKee's complaint in *New American State Papers: Indian Affairs,* Vol. 4: 158.

33. The treaty is in Kappler, comp., *Indian Affairs: Laws and Treaties*, 2: 39–45.

34. *New American State Papers: Indian Affairs,* Vol. 4: 175.

CHAPTER 6

1. Larry L. Nelson, ed., *A History of Jonathan Alder: His Captivity and Life with the Indians* (Akron: University of Akron Press, 2003), 16–17, 117.

2. Gregory Evans Dowd, *A Spirited Resistance: The North American Indian Struggle for Unity, 1745–1815* (Baltimore: Johns Hopkins University Press, 1992), 114.

3. John Johnston, *Recollections of Sixty Years on the Ohio Frontier* (1915; reprinted Van Buren, OH: The Eastern Frontier/R. E. Davis Co. Publishing, 2001), 11, 59.

4. Anthony F. C. Wallace, *Jefferson and the Indians: The Tragic Fate of the First Americans* (Cambridge: Harvard University Press, 1999), quote at 11; Reginald Horsman, *Expansion and American Indian Policy 1783–1812* (1967; reprinted Norman: University of Oklahoma Press, 1992).

5. Stephen Warren, *The Shawnees and Their Neighbors, 1795–1870* (Urbana: University of Illinois Press, 2005), ch. 3; Lawrence Kinnaird, ed., *Spain in the Mississippi Valley, 1765–1794: Translations of Materials from the Spanish Archives in the Bancroft Library*, Annual Report of the American Historical Association for 1945, part 2: 335; part 3: xxx, 25, 206.

6. Letter reprinted in Henry Harvey, *History of the Shawnee Indians* (Cincinnati: Ephraim Morgan and Sons, 1855), 129–31.

7. Francis Paul Prucha, ed., *Documents of United States Indian Policy* (Lincoln: University of Nebraska Press, 1975), 10, 22–23.

8. On Black Hoof's role during the last thirty years of his life, see R. David Edmunds, " 'A Watchful Safeguard to Our Habitations': Black Hoof and the Loyal Shawnees," in Frederick E. Hoxie, Ronald Hoffman, and Peter J. Albert, eds., *Native Americans in the Early Republic* (Charlottesville: University Press of Virginia, 1999), 162–99, and Warren, *The Shawnees and Their Neighbors*.

9. Edmunds, "A Watchful Safeguard," 167–69.

10. Paul A. Hutton, "William Wells: Frontier Scout and Indian Agent," *Indiana Magazine of History*, 74 (1978), 183–222; R. David Edmunds, " 'Evil Men Who Add to Our Difficulties': Shawnees, Quakers, and William Wells, 1807–1808," *American Indian Culture and Research Journal*, 14 (1990), 1–14; Gayle Thornbrough, ed., *Letter Book of the Indian Agency at Fort Wayne 1809–1815* (Indianapolis: Indiana Historical Society, 1961), 12–18.

11. Edmunds, " 'Evil Men Who Add to Our Difficulties,' " 6–7; Thornbrough, ed., *Letter Book of the Indian Agency at Fort Wayne*, 19, 34, 40–41.

12. Harvey, *History of the Shawnee Indians*, 140, 142.

13. Thornbrough, ed., *Letter Book of the Indian Agency at Fort Wayne*, 46–48; Edmunds, " 'Evil Men Who Add to Our Difficulties,' " 8–11.

CHAPTER 7

1. This chapter is indebted to two fine biographies of the brothers: John Sugden, *Tecumseh: A Life* (New York: Henry Holt, 1997), and R. David Edmunds, *The Shawnee Prophet* (Lincoln: University of Nebraska Press, 1983).

2. Quoted in Sugden, *Tecumseh*, 96, 198, 216.

3. John Johnston, *Recollections of Sixty Years on the Ohio Frontier* (1915; reprinted Van Buren, OH: The Eastern Frontier/R. E. Davis Co. Publishing, 2001), 12.

4. Sugden, *Tecumseh,* 22–23.

5. Johnston, *Recollections of Sixty Years on the Ohio Frontier,* 12.

6. Johnston, *Recollections of Sixty Years on the Ohio Frontier,* 13.

7. Edmunds, *The Shawnee Prophet*, 38.

8. Alfred A. Cave, *Prophets of the Great Spirit: Native American Revitalization Movements in Eastern North America* (Lincoln: University of Nebraska Press, 2006), 92–94.

9. Gregory Evans Dowd, *A Spirited Resistance: The North American Indian Struggle for Unity, 1745–1815* (Baltimore: Johns Hopkins University Press, 1992).

10. Edward Denning Andrews, "The Shaker Mission to the Shawnee Indians," *Winterthur Portfolio*, 7 (1972), 113–28, quote at 26. The missionaries recorded an account of the Prophet's teachings.

11. Clarence Edwin Carter, ed., *The Territorial Papers of the United States*, 28 vols. (Washington, DC: Government Printing Office, 1934–75), 7: 465–70, 498–99, 531, 540–41, 555–60.

12. Quoted in Dowd, *Spirited Resistance*, 145.

13. Stephen Warren, *The Shawnees and Their Neighbors, 1795–1870* (Urbana: University of Illinois Press, 2005), 31.

14. The Fort Wayne treaty is in Charles J. Kappler, comp., *Indian Affairs: Laws and Treaties*, 2 vols. (Washington, DC: Government Printing Office, 1904), 2: 101–3.

15. John Sugden, *Blue Jacket: Warrior of the Shawnees* (Lincoln: University of Nebraska Press, 2000), 256–57; Sugden, *Tecumseh*, quote at 187.

16. Sugden, *Tecumseh*, 198–202; Edmunds, *The Shawnee Prophet*, 90–92.

17. Public Record Office, C.O.42/351: 42–43.

18. Reginald Horsman, *Matthew Elliott, British Indian Agent* (Detroit: Wayne State University Press, 1964), 120, 146.

19. Quoted in Sugden, *Tecumseh*, 215.

20. Richard Drinnon, ed., *Memoirs of a Captivity among the Indians of North America by John Dunn Hunter* (New York: Schocken Books, 1973), 28.

21. Carl F. Klinck and James Talman, eds., *The Journal of Major John Norton 1816* (Toronto: The Champlain Society, 1970), 174–75.

22. Gayle Thornbrough, ed., *Letter Book of the Indian Agency at Fort Wayne 1809–1815* (Indianapolis: Indiana Historical Society, 1961), 162, 165; Carter, ed., *Territorial Papers of the United States*, 16: 252.

23. R. David Edmunds, " 'A Watchful Safeguard to Our Habitations': Black Hoof and the Loyal Shawnees," in Frederick E. Hoxie, Ronald Hoffman, and Peter J. Albert, eds., *Native Americans and the Early Republic* (Charlottesville: University Press of Virginia, 1999), 162–99, quote at 183.

24. Edmunds, " 'A Watchful Safeguard to Our Habitations,' " 186–87.

25. Tecumseh's speech is in Public Record Office, War Office Records, W.O.71/243: 381–82.

26. W.O.71/243: 11, 159.

27. The proceedings of Proctor's court-martial are in W.O. 71/243.

28. Guy St-Denis, *Tecumseh's Bones* (Montreal: McGill-Queens University Press, 2005).

29. Public Records Office, Foreign Office Records, F.O.5/119: 142–43.

CHAPTER 8

1. Stephen Warren, *The Shawnees and Their Neighbors, 1795–1870* (Urbana: University of Illinois Press, 2005).

2. Charles J. Kappler, comp., *Indian Affairs: Laws and Treaties*, 2 vols. (Washington, DC: Government Printing Office, 1904), 2: 145–52; Henry Harvey, *History of the Shawnee Indians* (Cincinnati: Ephraim Morgan and Sons, 1855), 258; Warren, *The Shawnees and Their Neighbors*, 56–59.

3. Figures given in James H. Howard, *Shawnee!: The Ceremonialism of a Native American Tribe and Its Cultural Background* (Athens: Ohio University Press, 1981), 32.

4. Warren, *The Shawnees and Their Neighbors*, 61.

5. John Johnston, *Recollections of Sixty Years on the Ohio Frontier* (1915; reprinted Van Buren, OH: The Eastern Frontier/R. E. Davis Co., 2001), 60.

6. Thomas Wildcat Alford, *Civilization and the Story of the Absentee Shawnees* (Norman: University of Oklahoma Press, 1936), 90.

7. Jerry Clark, *The Shawnee* (Lexington: University of Kentucky Press, 1977), 25.

8. A census of Indian tribes in Missouri listed 1,200 Shawnees on Apple River and near the Mississippi swamps in 1817; another census report compiled in 1822 listed 1,383 Shawnees in Missouri. Clarence E. Carter, ed., *The Territorial Papers of the United States* (Washington, DC: Government Printing Office, 1934–75), 15: 305.

9. John Mack Faragher, *Daniel Boone: The Life and Legend of an American Pioneer* (New York: Henry Holt, 1992), 313–14.

10. *American State Papers. Class II. Indian Affairs*, 2 vols. (Washington, DC: Gales and Seaton, 1834), 2: 11.

11. Kappler, comp., *Indian Affairs: Laws and Treaties* 2: 262–64.

12. R. David Edmunds, *The Shawnee Prophet* (Lincoln: University of Nebraska Press, 1983), ch. 8.

13. National Archives, Record Group 75, M234, reel 300: 51, 136, 138, 142. I am grateful to John Bowes for copies of these documents relating to Shawnee migrations and material culture.

14. Harvey, *History of the Shawnee Indians*, 145, 185, 212.

15. Kappler, comp., *Indian Affairs: Laws and Treaties* 2: 327–34.

16. Harvey, *History of the Shawnee Indians*, 185–89.

17. Warren, *The Shawnees and Their Neighbors*, 66–67.

18. Harvey, *History of the Shawnee Indians,* 215–16, 221–29; Carl G. Klopfenstein, "Westward Ho: Removal of Ohio Shawnees, 1832–1833," *Bulletin of the Historical and Philosophical Society of Ohio*, 15 (1957), 3–31; Gardiner quote at 16.

19. Quoted in Klopfenstein, "Westward Ho: Removal of Ohio Shawnees," 12; "Removal of Indians from Ohio: Dunihue Correspondence of 1832," *Indiana Magazine of History*, 35 (1939), 411, 415.

20. Harvey, *History of the Shawnee Indians*, 230–31; "Removal of Indians from Ohio: Dunihue Correspondence of 1832," 423–24; Gardiner quoted in Klopfenstein, "Westward Ho: Removal of Ohio Shawnees," 18.

21. Harvey, *History of the Shawnee Indians*, 230–38.

22. Gary Clayton Anderson, *The Conquest of Texas: Ethnic Cleansing in the Promised Land, 1820–1875* (Norman: University of Oklahoma Press, 2005).

23. H. Allen Anderson, "The Delaware and Shawnee Indians and the Republic of Texas, 1820–1845," *Southwestern Historical Quarterly*, 94 (1990–91), 231–60.

24. Carter, ed., *Territorial Papers of the United States*, 14: 197–98, 313, 316, 412; 19: 347, 438, 581; Warren, *The Shawnees and Their Neighbors*, 84–95; John P. Bowes, *Exiles and Pioneers: Eastern Indians in the Trans-Mississippi West* (Cambridge: Cambridge University Press, 2007), ch. 4.

25. Randolph B. Marcy, *The Prairie Traveler: A Handbook for Overland Expeditions* (New York: Harper and Brothers, 1859), 183–86.

26. Bowes, *Exiles and Pioneers*, chs. 4–5; Warren, *The Shawnees and Their Neighbors*, chs. 4–5.

27. Harvey, *History of the Shawnee Indians*, 269–70.

28. Joab Spencer, "The Shawnee Indians," *Transactions of the Kansas State Historical Society*, 10 (1908): 382–402, quote at 387.

29. Harvey, *History of the Shawnee Indians*, 273–74; Warren, *The Shawnees and Their Neighbors*, 150–51.

30. Harvey, *History of the Shawnee Indians*, 288.

31. Alford, *Civilization and the Story of the Absentee Shawnees*, 80–81, 173–76.

32. Howard, *Shawnee!*, 20–22; Charles Callender, "Shawnee," in Bruce G. Trigger, ed., *Handbook of North American Indians, Volume 15: Northeast* (Washington, DC: Smithsonian Institution, 1978), 632–34; Warren, *The Shawnees and Their Neighbors*, 170–71.

33. http://www.astribe.com/Government.html.

AFTERWORD

1. Frederick Jackson Turner, *The Frontier in American History* (New York: Holt, 1920).

2. Elizabeth A. Perkins, *Border Life: Experience and Memory in the Revolutionary Ohio Valley* (Chapel Hill: University of North Carolina Press, 1998), 173.

3. Thomas Wildcat Alford, *Civilization and the Story of the Absentee Shawnees* (Norman: University of Oklahoma Press, 1936), 111, 167.

BIBLIOGRAPHY

Interested readers should consult the notes for additional sources.

Alford, Thomas Wildcat, *Civilization and the Story of the Absentee Shawnees* (Norman: University of Oklahoma Press, 1936).

Aron, Stephen, *How the West Was Lost: The Transformation of Kentucky from Daniel Boone to Henry Clay* (Baltimore: Johns Hopkins University Press, 1996).

Bowes, John P., *Exiles and Pioneers: Eastern Indians in the Trans-Mississippi West* (Cambridge: Cambridge University Press, 2007).

Calloway, Colin G., *The American Revolution in Indian Country* (Cambridge: Cambridge University Press, 1995).

Cave, Alfred A., *Prophets of the Great Spirit: Native American Revitalization Movements in Eastern North America* (Lincoln: University of Nebraska Press, 2006).

Clark, Jerry E., *The Shawnee* (Lexington: University Press of Kentucky, 1993).

Dowd, Gregory Evans, *A Spirited Resistance: The North American Indian Struggle for Unity, 1745–1815* (Baltimore: Johns Hopkins University Press, 1992).

Edmunds, R. David, *Tecumseh and the Quest for Indian Leadership* (Boston: Little, Brown, and Co., 1984).

Edmunds, R. David, *The Shawnee Prophet* (Lincoln: University of Nebraska Press, 1983).

Faragher, John Mack, *Daniel Boone, The Life and Legend of an American Pioneer* (New York: Henry Holt, 1992).

Gilbert, Bill, *God Gave Us This Country: Tekamthi and the First American Civil War* (New York: Atheneum, 1989).

Harvey, Henry, *History of the Shawnee Indians, from the Year 1681 to 1854* (Cincinnati: Ephraim Morgan and Sons, 1855).

Horsman, Reginald, *Matthew Elliott, British Indian Agent* (Detroit: Wayne State University Press, 1964).

Howard, James H., *Shawnee!: The Ceremonialism of a Native American Tribe and Its Cultural Background* (Athens: Ohio University Press, 1981).

Kinietz, Vernon, and Voegelin, Erminie W., eds., *Shawnese Traditions: C. C. Trowbridge's Account* (Ann Arbor: University of Michigan, 1939).

Klinck, Carl F., ed., *Tecumseh: Fact and Fiction in Early Records* (Englewood Cliffs, NJ: Prentice-Hall, 1961).

Klopfenstein, Carl G., "Westward Ho: Removal of Ohio Shawnees, 1832–1833," *Bulletin of the Historical and Philosophical Society of Ohio*, 15 (1957), 3–31.

McConnell, Michael N., *A Country Between: The Upper Ohio Valley and Its Peoples, 1724–1774* (Lincoln: University of Nebraska Press, 1992).

Nelson, Larry L., *A Man of Distinction Among Them: Alexander McKee and the Ohio Country Frontier, 1754–1799* (Kent, OH: Kent State University Press, 1999).

Noe, Randolph, *The Shawnee Indians: An Annotated Bibliography* (Lanham, MD: The Scarecrow Press, Inc., 2001).

O'Donnell, James H., III, *Ohio's First Peoples* (Athens: Ohio University Press, 2004).

Perkins, Elizabeth A., *Border Life: Experience and Memory in the Revolutionary Ohio Valley* (Chapel Hill: University of North Carolina Press, 1998).

Sugden, John, *Blue Jacket: Warrior of the Shawnees* (Lincoln: University of Nebraska Press, 2000).

Sugden, John, *Tecumseh* (New York: Henry Holt, 1997).

Sugden, John, *Tecumseh's Last Stand* (Norman: University of Oklahoma Press, 1985).

Sword, Wiley, *President Washington's War: The Struggle for the Old Northwest, 1790–1795* (Norman: University of Oklahoma Press, 1985).

Tanner, Helen Hornbeck, *Atlas of Great Lakes Indian History* (Norman: University of Oklahoma Press, 1987).

Thom, Dark Rain, and Thom, James Alexander, *Warrior Woman: A Novel Based on the Life of Nonhelema, Shawnee Woman Chief* (New York: Ballantine Books, 2003).

Warren, Stephen, *The Shawnees and Their Neighbors, 1795–1870* (Urbana: University of Illinois Press, 2005).

INDEX

Page numbers in *italics* refer to picture captions.